FROM PERDITION TO SALVATION

The Life and Times of a Convert

A Place For All Ministries

Chaplain Shane "Rev" MacQuarrie

ISBN: 979-8-89663-095-1

Contents

Introduction

I have been prompted to write this, yet I have no idea if anyone will ever read it. This is not your typical story; it is one of a man who lived a selfish and irredeemable life, yet somewhere along the way, I found the greatest truth in the world. Once I found that, I never looked back or regretted the choices I made from that day on.

Much of my childhood is clouded in mystery. I have very few memories of my early days. There are things I remember, things I have been told, and things I think I remember. They are all jumbled up, and I am rarely sure which of these three categories they fit into.

Here are a few of them:

I remember playing tag in our house with several kids from the neighborhood. We would climb into the rafters in the garage, moving as quickly as possible to avoid being tagged. No one was hurt doing this.

When my brother was about 5 or 6 years old, my friends and I got our ball stuck in a tree in our front yard. The lowest branch was too high to use to climb the tree, so I tossed a baseball bat up into the branches, attempting to dislodge our ball. I did not see my brother near us. When the bat came down, it hit my brother in the face. I got into a lot of trouble over that.

I have a newspaper article from my father's time in San Diego. They had a family day at the base, and there is a picture of me behind a 50 cal. I do not remember the day, but I have physical evidence of it in that picture. I also have a picture of my sister and I, with our father, at his graduation from the Citadel Academy. I had my tonsils removed when I was young. Again, I know that this happened but I have no recollection of these events.

Finally, when I was in junior high, I went out to ride my skateboard one day. At the top of our driveway, it got stuck on a small rock. The normal move to dislodge the rock is to rock the skateboard and then continue on the way. You do this by rocking it backward, then jumping it forward, which will typically dislodge the rock. I have done this several times before. This time, however, my skateboard jumped out from underneath me, shooting out into the street. I fell. I also tried to catch myself in the fall. This caused me to break my right wrist. It broke at a diagonal and then snapped back so that my hand was resting above my wrist. I made it inside the house and called Gail, a friend's mom, who took me to the hospital.

At this point, my mom and David were already divorced. David had medical authority for me to receive service at the hospital, so we had to wait for him to arrive and sign off on permission for them to set my arm. In the meantime, they put a brace on my hand, strapping it to a bar, and a weight on my arm, which they used to separate the bone, which had already begun to heal and fuse together. I laughed most of the time, waiting for them to be able to set the break and put a cast on it.

The first cast was a plaster cast. At some point, before school let out for the summer, I got into a minor skirmish with another student. I hit him with my cast, which caused it to break again. This time, they had to pin my arm and put me in a fiberglass cast. This would be much cooler in the summer. I used a coat hanger to scratch my arm inside the cast. I lost so much mass in my arm that I could slide a couple of fingers into it and twist the metal pin in my wrist when it itched. Feeling the metal turn in the bone was an interesting sensation.

A final memory I have is when I was around 12 - 13 years old. A few friends and I went out to see a movie at Montclair Mall. I have no idea what movie it was, but there were four of us. It was either before or after the movie, but we were walking in the parking lot. My friend Pete saw a group of guys approaching us. I did not notice that the three of them turned and headed a different way, and this group of young black men came upon me in a pack. One of them said something to me, not threatening, just a quiet remark. It was at this point that he punched me on the side of the head, dropping me. Two or three of those in the pack then kicked me in the back as they all took off running. I was no worse for wear; I just had my bell rung for a second and then got up and finished my time with my friends. Pete made a remark that he expected me to fight them off because I was taking Taekwondo at the time. I told him that had I tried to fight, I would have gotten beaten much worse. The numbers were not on my side.

My younger years were spent playing outside with friends, reading sci-fi and fantasy books, and playing Dungeons & Dragons with friends. Some of the books I enjoyed reading include Elf Quest comics, Dragon Lance books, the Lord of the Rings series, and Piers Anthony's Incarnations of

Immortality. I was a dork who would become a social outcast by my own choices. As I grew, my social circle shrank.

I knew about God but never knew God until much later in my life. Many members of my family knew I was not a Christian, but none of them tried to share the gospel message with me. Looking back on my life, I wish someone had at least tried to reach me. Maybe this is why I am so passionate about sharing the gospel with others.

My Early Years

I was born on a Thursday in the previous century. This has extraordinarily little bearing on anything else, and I honestly have no memory of it, but it was still a Thursday. Much of my childhood is a blur, mostly given form by what others have told me. My mother told me that she filed for divorce from my father before I was even born. I spent much of my youth wondering if either of them even wanted me. My mother was married three times and divorced twice by the time I was five years old. My father was her first marriage and divorce. From my mom, I have a sister, who is two years older than me, and a brother, who is five years younger than me.

My dad gave me two younger sisters (three in total from him), who were both born after I was twelve. One of them was born in the States, and I got to spend a summer with her when she was younger. His youngest was born in Greece, while my father was stationed there. I did not meet her until many years later. My dad passed away when I was 23 years old.

My life was one of turmoil and constant change. I did not grow up in the Church, but I went every other weekend when I was with my father's parents. Because my dad was a Marine, he would be stationed or deployed all over the world. Because of this, to stay connected with his side of the family, my older sister and I spent every other weekend with our paternal grandparents. Grandma and grandpa were members of the United Methodist Church. Spending my weekends with them was the only time I was exposed to Jesus.

Most of my good memories involve my paternal grandparents. I enjoyed going to church with them when we visited, and I would assume that my sister did, too. Our little brother did not go with us because his dad was not our dad. It always felt weird to me, but he had his own grandma, who we would all visit. Maybe David, his dad, was uncomfortable with the idea of sending his son to spend the weekend with people he did not know?

During these weekends with our grandparents, we would play cards, I would get a haircut with my grandfather, and we might go to the park or to some other event. Mostly, it was spent with them. It was the closest I ever felt to being happy. During the holidays, my dad's family would all gather at their house. This meant I got to see my cousins, Jared and Christy. Jared was a couple of weeks older than me, and Christy was just a bit older than my sister, so we got to play together like old friends. Christmas was probably the worst, though. Because we were so close in age, we would often receive the same gift. This meant that Jared and I had to open the same gift at the same time. It was also what formed my love for the holidays. We got to see family members who were not always close by. It was a time of love and family – exactly what makes the holidays so special. My grandmother was an amazing cook, so there was that.

When I was five years old, my little brother was born. At this point, we were living in Ontario, California. My mom and David had just bought a nice little 3-bedroom house. There were plenty of kids in the neighborhood. My earliest friend was Pete G. He lived just down the street from us, on a corner.

Pete and I remained close until probably 6th grade. It was at this point that our interests drifted apart, but we remained in contact until I joined the Navy after high school. I still talk to his mom through Facebook.

In addition to Pete, I had a few other friends. Kelly, Mike, Mike, Joey, Robbie, and several others lived in the neighborhood. We were all within a few years of each other. Most of our parents knew each other as well. During the summers, we would have neighborhood BBQs and play volleyball in the cul-de-sac at the end of the street on which we lived. Kim and her family had a pool in their backyard where many of us would swim during the summer.

This was in the 80s, and we were latchkey kids. For those of you not familiar with this term, it meant that we kids had a house key and a general rule to be home when the streetlights came on. The rest of the time, we were mainly left to our own devices. We would ride our bikes around the neighborhood, fashioning ramps out of spare wood and blocks or bricks. We would play tag at whoever's house had no parents and generally got into mischief all summer long. We had chores to do, but once they were done, we were on our own. Some of the kids, Pete and Kelly, had rules about not playing outside until after 12 on Saturdays, but not our family. We were free to come and go if we left a note and were quiet.

It was common for our parents to send us to the store; I was probably 8 or 9 at the time, with a note to purchase alcohol or cigarettes. The store owner had no problem letting us do this, and it was only about 1-1 ½ mile walk each way. On our way, we could go to 7-11 and get a Slurpee, so we were always up for the trip. I remember pushing the lawnmower up to the gas station across the street from there to get gas so I could mow the lawn. Gas was 75.9 cents a gallon back then.

Most summers, my sister and I would spend with our father. If he were local, meaning in Southern California, we would see him every other weekend, but if he were across the country, we would typically fly out for several weeks during the summer. I remember spending summers with my dad in Georgia and Virginia. I enjoyed these times because I got to see my father and spend time with him doing "boy stuff."

David and my mom separated during my elementary years, 4th or 5th grade. I continued to live in the house with my mom and her string of boyfriends. She had one more marriage after David, but it was very short-lived, and he left her in a ton of debt after falsifying her signature on several loan documents. In my 6th grade year, I lived with David and my brother in the house. His girlfriend and her family came along with David. It was insane. This was a 3-bedroom home with a den, and I ended up sleeping in the master bedroom with David and my brother. Her family took over the other rooms, including the den. We had 6 adults, my brother and I, her daughter who was my age, and a toddler all living in this house. I began to spend even more time away from home. This was also when I began to develop a drinking habit.

As we got older, we began to venture out to the mall. This was always a lot of fun for us kids. Mostly, it was window shopping unless we had money left over from birthdays, Christmas, or our allowance. Then we could buy the cool stuff our parents never would. Cassette tapes and books were the main items for me. I was not addicted to fashion at this point; I just enjoyed my music and reading. I was probably in 5th or 6th grade when I discovered the Dragonlance series. The mall was a wonderful place to meet up with friends from school, especially those who did not live near you, and just spend time having fun. We could meet up to see a movie, hang out at the food court, and just be teens. It was a fun time.

In the summer of 1984, I went to visit my dad in Quantico. My sister had spent the school year with him, so I spent that summer with him by myself. That year, the Olympic Games were being held in Los Angeles, so I was happy to get out of California. My dad and I spent a lot of time together. He still had to work during the week, but on the weekends, we went to tour several Revolutionary and Civil War sites. I learned a lot about history on those excursions and picked up some meaning and memorabilia. We also took a weekend trip to Washington, D.C. I got two souvenirs from there. One was a T-shirt with the Olympic rings on it; one set off to the side. The caption on the shirt read, "Let the Russians play with themselves." The reason for this was that Russia had decided to boycott the Olympic games that year, but the US had boycotted the games in 1980, so I guess it was a fair trade. The other item was a set of four gold coins to commemorate the Olympics.

I wore the T-shirt to school one day, and my teacher felt that it was inappropriate. She demanded that I turn it inside out for the day and never wear it to school again. She felt that it had a sexual meaning rather than a true meaning. I got a one-day suspension a few weeks later when I wore it again. I was that kind of a jerk.

It was also in my 6th grade year that I met Jeremy C and was introduced to the joys of Dungeons & Dragons. I had been reading fantasy novels and comics for some time, but role-playing was something else altogether. I began spending almost every weekend over at Jeremy's. A couple of other guys and we would get together, Jeremy's mom would order us pizza, and we would stay up most of the night playing D&D. Occasionally, we would head over to John's house, where we would do the same thing, but alcohol was involved.

John was a Navy veteran; I was never sure of his discharge status. John stayed at home as a caregiver for his sick uncle. I always had a problem with how John treated his uncle, but I never said anything because I was just a kid. John was verbally abusive to his uncle, who was unable to take care of himself at all or even verbalize his needs to anyone. This would allow John to close the bedroom door and leave his uncle to suffer in his own filth, while John did just about anything else. John was over 21, and yes, I should have been cautious about someone his age wanting to spend time with kids in junior high, but it never really crossed my mind. Nothing ever happened that I am aware of, but it still should have been a huge red flag for the rest of us. On the weekends that we spent with John, I would typically go through a fifth of Bacardi 151 over the weekend.

My sister and I attended Vernon Junior High. She graduated from junior high the year before I started. In California, at the time, junior high was 7th & 8th grade. The main street, Mountain

Ave, was the dividing line for the schools. Everyone on our side of the Mountain went to Vernon. Several of my friends lived on the other side, though, which meant that they went to a different junior high. We could still spend time together after school and on the weekends, but it also meant that it was harder to keep up with each other. Jeremy went to the other school.

My Teen Years

After junior high, my sister and I attended Ontario High School. It seemed like half of the students came from Vernon Junior High and the other half from the other junior high, but not all the students from both went to Ontario. Jeremy ended up going to Montclair High, along with some other friends. I have always been in advanced classes. I tended to learn concepts quickly and was able to absorb inputs from multiple sources at the same time. Most of my friends were not in these same classes. This meant that many of my new classmates in the *Gifted and Talented Education (GATE)* classes had come from the other junior high. I did not know them and did not fit in very well. I felt that they were all *nerds*, which they proved in our English class at the beginning of the semester. Our English teacher decided that she wanted to share a joke with the class. It was about a snail buying a new car. He wanted all the emblems replaced with a large "S." As the snail drove off the lot, the salesman expressed the punchline: "Look at that S car go (escargot)." Dumb joke, right? Well, the whole class burst out in laughter at it while I sat there in my chair, lamenting its stupidity.

Not long after this, we had an earthquake. Now, California uses portable classrooms on many of its campuses. The population simply grew faster than the schools could keep up. This also meant that these "buildings" were less sturdy than the regular classrooms. Our English class was in one such room. During that earthquake, I saw one of the most spectacular moves ever. The earthquake hit while our teacher was sitting at the front of her desk, addressing the class. The floor was "rolling," which means that you could see and feel the roll of the seismic wave across the floor. Our teacher performed a backflip across her desk, one hand on the desk and the other moving her chair behind the desk out of the way, as she slipped under her desk without touching the floor until she was under it. It was amazing to see. The class was sitting there in stunned silence at what we had just seen until the teacher stuck her head up from under her desk and told us to *duck and cover*. It was cool to see.

Now, all my classes except for Physical Education were part of the *GATE* program. This means that all the students should have had exceptional IQs. This is the program for the intellectuals of our school. Or at least that is what they told us. After the earthquake incident, several of the smartest students came out and tried to figure out if it had been a real earthquake or if the school had placed something under the portables to simulate the effects of an earthquake for more realistic drills. I applaud their thinking, but the cost of something like that would not be feasible for schools to do. And they should have known that.

One day, early in my freshman year, I was sitting in my Social Studies class reading a book. The problem is that I was reading a Dragon Lance book while the teacher was teaching. Oh, and I was turned sideway in my seat, hunched over reading, not even trying to hide it. The teacher decided to call me out for reading, as he should have. But when he tried to prove his point by asking me what HE had been saying, I gave the highlights of his discussion on Neanderthal man and the bones of Lucy being found. He was not impressed by my ability to sum up in less than 5 minutes what he had taken 20 minutes to explain. He then asked me if I thought his class was boring, to which I answered in the affirmative. He was understandably upset by my answer and sent me to the office. After his class was over, he came up to join my counselor and me in order to find a different class schedule for me. I did not care because now I would be back in *regular* classes with my friends.

One of the classes that got switched was my English class. The teacher was a little quirky but nice enough. For some reason, she liked me, not in that way, you sicko. I cannot say that the feeling was mutual, though. She made it clear to the class that she was a Christian. This was back when you could still do that. During a class discussion, I began to dissect many of the "inaccuracies and contradictions" in the Bible. I brought this poor woman to tears and laughed about it. I was a horrible person and felt no remorse about it.

I had a few girlfriends in high school, but nothing serious. I was not as experienced as most of my friends, apparently, who all boasted of their conquests. They were all more outgoing than I was. I was meek and shy. I played some sports when I was younger, such as soccer and baseball, but I was never exceptionally good at them. I enjoyed riding my 12-speed and did so often in my teens. I used to ride about 100 miles per day on the weekends.

In my freshman year in high school, I began wrestling. I was going to try out for the soccer team, a sport I really enjoyed, but a friend convinced me that I would never make it because

I was not Hispanic. We went out and watched many of the guys on the team play one weekend, just for fun, and those guys were a LOT better than I was, so I let him talk me into joining the wrestling team. I was not a limp fish on the mat, but I had a long way to go to gain the skills and experience needed for this sport. Sadly, I wrestled many varsity matches that year, not because I was that good but rather because the senior in my weight class had trouble making the grades for academic eligibility. About half of my matches were against Juniors and Seniors for other schools.

In the second month of my sophomore year, my mom and I moved out of the house we had lived in since I was 5. We moved into an apartment in a different city and county. I began attending my second school that year, close to Halloween. Now, I have always been comfortable in jeans and a T-shirt. This is exactly what I wore every day. My time here, this time, was limited. I began my third high school that year in April. My mom decided to move back to Ontario because she thought I was unhappy living so far away from my friends. The thing is, I had just started darting Susan right before we moved. She was a Senior, and I called her Schoen, which is German for "beautiful." We met in our German 2 class. She and I went to prom that year, but it was a lack luster event because neither of us was driving at that time, and she was more than a little weird.

At my third school, I had to use my sister's home address to register. My mom did this because the school I would have attended, based on where we lived, had their year extended out due to some wildfires at the beginning of the year. Rather than having my year dragged out, she registered me at another school. It was there that I met Kim. She was a senior (noticing a trend here?) with whom I had a couple of classes. I would typically walk her home and then head over to my sister's house to get my bike and ride home. One day, Kim asked me to go with her to a job interview. The manager asked me if I was looking for work too, and so he hired both of us, but not before making sure that she and I were not dating. I stayed there for a couple of months, which was longer than Kim. At one point, we were considering going steady, but that never went anywhere. That summer, my mom and I moved back to Fullerton so I could attend Buena Park High again. Not sure why, but my mom never consulted me in any of her decisions.

At my first high school, the student population was primarily Hispanic, and many of them did not like white people. Because of this, I became associated with a group of people I had never met – skinheads. I was unapologetic about who I was as I tried to find myself. I typically wore ripped jeans, a t-shirt, a leather biker jacket, a bandana on my head, and my Doc Martins. I looked like a typical skinhead, except my hair would frequently fluctuate between bald and long. This is the year that I met Jack. Jack was a good friend and was your typical white trash-kid. The yard at his house was full of broken-down vehicles, he smoked more than I did, and his house was dirty, but he was a fun guy to hang around with. He and I would typically go surfing at the beach before school and hang out in the evenings. He was in the high school band.

Now, Buena Park, being primarily Hispanic, also had a local gang – Eastside Buena Park. I guess some of them had an issue with how I dressed and decided to try and make trouble for me at school. One day, as I was walking down the hall at school, a bunch of them decided to come at me in a group. All they did was run into me and jostle me around. No one was hurt. I do not remember what they said, but I had a discussion with Jack. Jack knew some of the shot-callers for the gang. He made a couple of phone calls, and that was the last of my problems with them. After that, the next time they saw me in the hallway, it was like Moses parting the Red Sea. They split right down the middle and gave me a wide berth on either side.

Jack was also the reason I met Jodie and Lisa. Jodie was a freshman on the drill team. For some reason, even though I was interested in Lisa, Jodie decided she liked me and let me know it at every turn. Jodie and I began dating not long after. Lisa began dating my cousin, Jared, not long after that. We would go to the movies, dinner, and special nights at Disneyland. AMC used to sponsor SoCal resident nights all the time, and she and I went to Homecoming together. Both were short-term relationships. Not sure what happened between Jared and Lisa, but Jodie began seeing someone else while still with me. She grew increasingly distant until I finally had other people telling me that she was dating some other guy. He tried to prove his physical superiority, which failed. There were three of them and one of me. He and I never exchanged words or blows, but his one friend who charged me went down, hard, in the hallway. End of relationship.

It was while dating Jody that I almost had a gun pulled on me. We were at a party at one of her friend's apartment. It was in a less-than-desirable neighborhood in Anaheim. There was a lot of drinking involved, so I spent most of my time outside.

See, by this point in my life, I had already decided that I did not like to drink, especially when I was going to be driving. After years of being a loner, I was uncomfortable around large groups and hated loud noises. Because of this, I was either chilling out on the hood of my car in the parking lot or inside the apartment for a few brief moments. Some would call me anti-social.

Jody's friend was dating someone older, and it had soured. I found out later that he was 21 years old. Her (ex)boyfriend showed up at the apartment, and they had a shouting match through the door. She eventually opened the door, and the shouting continued. I was on the hood of my car, less than 50 feet away. Somewhere along the way, Jody got involved in the argument. I was not worried because she could handle herself. Well, this guy decided to push her, which was my breaking point. I quickly came in and positioned myself between him and the two girls. I eventually had him back up against the railing on the landing in front of the apartment. I basically told him to jump if he felt froggy. The whole time, he had his right hand at his back. I knew that he had something, I honestly expected a knife and was trying to keep the distance close to limit his options. I was close enough that I could grab his arm long before he could bring any type of weapon to bear on me. When the police showed up, the guy was arrested for carrying an unlicensed firearm in his pack pocket. This was one of the first times that I wished to inflict massive harm upon another person. Why didn't he pull the gun he had?

At the end of my Junior year, I began dating Lisa. She and I had remained close friends, and she made the first move by grabbing me and kissing me as I walked her to class. Told you I was a shy guy. She would come over to my apartment most weekends but never spent the night. It bummed me out at the time. She was a senior. That summer, she went to Europe with her aunt and uncle while I stayed home, worked, and surfed. She came home at the end of the summer, and we broke up shortly after that.

After she and I broke up, my friend Jack invited me to go to church with him. I was still practicing Wicca and Druidry at the time, but I had nothing better to do on Wednesday night, so I went. It was there that I met Angel. Angel was a friend of Jack's girlfriend. Jack bet me that I wouldn't ask Angela out. So, for the next couple of weeks, while Jack was driving the bus to pick up kids for the Wednesday night service and youth group, I would ride along with him. Angel was already riding the bus, and it gave us a chance to talk and get to know each other. She made it clear that she would not date someone who was not going to church, so I began to go to church, even if only to see her.

We began dating, which did not thrill her parents. I was driving by this time so I could go to her house and see her or even pick her up for dates. We would typically go to dinner and a movie or just hang out wherever. I was in and out of my mom's apartment due to ongoing issues with her and me being rebellious. It was there that my friend Jason gave me my first tattoo. It was done with a homemade tattoo gun: a motor from a Walkman cassette player, mechanical pencil, and guitar string, and powered by two AA batteries. Jason did one tattoo on each of my shoulders. The string broke while tattooing my last name on my right shoulder. This made Angel queasy. I asked her to go to the prom with me, but she thought I was joking. I wish she had gone with me. We continued dating until after I had joined the military.

In my senior year of high school, I worked at a telemarketing company. The pay was decent, but the atmosphere was not healthy. Most of us smoked and drank too much coke or coffee. I worked the evening shift, occasionally coming in earlier to try and get a few more calls placed. We were paid by the hour or commission, which ever was higher. Our commission was based on qualified calls who attended the entirety of our 90-minute sales seminar for a time-share. Yes, I was that guy who would interrupt your dinner to try and book you into a high pressured sales pitch. Most of us would come and go in this business, often leaving to try something new and then coming back because of how much we could make at this job. I worked for a few months at SportCO but would often come back to Alladin Tour & Travel (AT&T). AT&T gave me the opportunity to work in the evenings and afford to take my girlfriend out afterward. We could not call after 9 PM, and many people stopped answering after 8, so we could get out and see a movie or have dinner. Having this level of freedom and flexibility was perfect for a young man with a girlfriend.

Early Religious Experience

I mentioned earlier that I was not raised in the Church, but I was exposed to the Church. However, I was about as far as possible from being a follower of Jesus. By the time I was 12, I was heavily influenced by fantasy stories; I played Dungeons & Dragons and began to investigate Druids. I would buy books, study everything I could about them, and even begin practicing rituals. New Age stores became one of my favorite hangouts when I was not in school or with friends playing D&D. By the time I was fifteen, I began getting into some more serious stuff and practicing Wicca. Through one of the stores, I found a local coven and began to learn from them.

Druidry is the practice of ancestral worship through invoking the power of the spirits of your ancestors and those native to your local area. It is nature-based and seeks to increase and improve your life through holistic teachings. We would use natural remedies rather than looking to pharmaceutical companies for treatment of ailments. If you have trouble sleeping, you could use Valerian root or Passionflower as natural sedatives to help you relax and sleep. Some of these worked, while others were less effective. We could also be classified as environmentalists. We valued nature and saw it as a responsibility. We needed to preserve nature (Mother Nature, after all) and seek to cause as little harm as possible.

When you read Celtic myths, you see the interactions between humans and nature. According to their mythology, the world was created when an egg hatched, creating the entire cosmos. From that egg, we got Danu (mother earth) and the sky god. It was the union of these two that created the Tuath De Danann, the giants and the monsters of the world. The Tuath are known as the Children of Danu. They eventually came to the Celtic shores, where they battled the Fomorians (monsters and giants). During their battles, many on both sides were killed. Eventually, the Tuath won out and exiled the Fomorians who still lived.

All the Tuath and Fomorians were identified with nature and had aspects of the natural world that they were to have exemplified. The Dagda was the greatest of them, but he did not rule unopposed or even unilaterally. Other Tuath would speak council and would even take over during certain events. They were much like other pagan religions of the time.

Eventually, man came to the shores of the Celtic lands. When man arrived, the Tuath knew that their time was limited. Rather than waging another war and losing more of their kind, they retreated into the Sidhe mounds that litter the Emerald Isle. As part of the agreement, mankind was to honor them and pay tribute to them at certain festival times throughout the year. It is here that we begin to see legends of Leprechauns, Elves, Dwarves, and other fantasy creatures. These all belong to the Tuath. The druidic rituals sought to pay tribute to the spirits of the Tuath in the area, seek out their favor for crops and hunting, and rid the world of evil. The Celtic religion dates to roughly 1200 BC and some organizations claim to have an unbroken line back to these earliest beliefs, but I found out that this was as wrong as I was.

Wicca is a similar story. Many covens will claim to have an unbroken line back to pre-Christian days, but Wicca is a creation of Gerald Gardner in the 50s. In 1951, England repealed their anti-witchcraft laws. This allowed people to begin to openly practice witchcraft. Gerald Gardner is recognized as the "father of modern Wicca." Many of his beliefs were influenced through his association with more controversial figures like Aleister Crowley, Freemasonry, and the Order of the Golden Dawn. Many of the theories and ideas he espoused have been thoroughly discredited since his death.

Wicca is a form of ceremonial magic based more on rituals and the raising of power and energy. Their covens are often overseen by both a priest and a priestess, but often, the high priestess will hold more power and sway than the priest. Today, many associate Wicca with sex-magic, and many of their rituals would culminate in a symbolic sex act, but that was not the point of it. They view the combining of male and female energy as the ultimate form of raising energy.

Druids would request aid from the spirits to make their will manifest, Wiccans would raise energy and ask that it make their will manifest, while witches would use spells and force their will to be made manifest. All three share some similarities, especially to the layman, but how each of them goes about getting their way in the world is slightly different.

I was involved with both a coven and grove in California and Washington. Even during the time that I was in the military, I served in various capacities. While on a cruise, I would often read tarot cards for some of my shipmates. I would honor the lunar festivals, even in foreign countries where I could go to jail or be killed. Occasionally, I would be contacted to perform a cleansing, or exorcism, for someone having trouble banishing something they summoned. This was my calling in the New Age.

When I was eighteen, I had a roommate I lived with. He was a friend of mine. I knew his wife, but not well. She came to me one night with an Ouija board that had been in her family for years. They had tried to get rid of it several times. Every time they threw it away, it would end up on the doorstep the next morning. She did not know what to do, but it scared her. She and I were talking about this, and I asked her to bring it to me. She brought it to me the next day, and then her husband and she went out for the night. That night, I performed a ritual to summon the spirit in the board and then exorcise it from its home. During the ritual, the candle I was burning exploded, throwing melted wax everywhere. After I was done, the board was just a board and broken in half. That was the last time we saw the board.

While stationed in San Diego, I brought my tarot cards with me. One time, I brought them out on training maneuvers and performed several readings for friends and shipmates. None of these really stood out to me as anything special, except for one. A friend of mine grew quiet while I was reading the cards. Turns out that I had just given him the rundown of the last couple of years of his life, and it scared him that I had mentioned things I should not have known. He did not talk to me for several days after that.

Another friend of mine was a member of the Satanic Temple. He would go out on the weekends, stay at the local

YMCA in downtown San Diego, and dress up like a Catholic priest. From there, he would venture out to bars and proceed to get drunk. He thought it was hilarious. He and I spent a lot of time together, working on rituals and just enjoying each other's company. I miss him sometimes and pray that he establishes a relationship with Christ. But back then, neither of us was interested in Jesus except as a punchline to joke or as an article of ridicule.

Throughout my life, I have seen spirits and demons. Some will call these "shadow people" and write them off as hallucinations, but I disagree. Some of these encounters have included feelings of dread, while others have been full of temptations and desires. I have had encounters that offered me everything I ever desired: money, women, position, and authority, many of which I was already working toward. Others left me sweating profusely, shaking, and unable to sleep for days with the visions that I had.

Military Service

After graduating high school, I joined the Navy. In September of that year, I went off to the Great Lakes Recruit Training Center. I spent the next several weeks learning military discipline and history. I had a little trouble there but came out with discipline and a desire to succeed in life. It was the first time I had been away from family for a prolonged period. Angela and I wrote letters back and forth, and after graduating, I returned to California for about a week before I headed off to Virginia for A-School. Before I left, she gave me her father's wedding band as a promise that she and I would be married after she graduated. That did not happen. We broke up because of rumors being spread about me and because I might have gotten someone else pregnant before I joined the Navy while she and I were dating. I found out many years later that I was not the father, but I still think of Ariel as my daughter, and I love her as one of my own.

During my time in the Navy, I went on two Western Pacific (WestPac) cruises, which would take us from the States to the Middle East by way of Asia or even Australia. We never made it to Australia, but we did spend a lot of time in Asia and Africa. On our first cruise, we went to Somalia to provide humanitarian relief, then to Hong Kong, Singapore, and finally to Dubai. I fell in love with Dubai while we were there.

In Hong Kong, we would anchor out in the bay and take a ferry ride into the port. While there, I found a bar that I would frequent. The main reason I went was the women who worked there. The sad truth of Hong Kong is that many of these young ladies were working girls. They would dance on a stage at these bars, and the patrons could pay for their company. If you paid the bar charge, you could then take these women to a hotel for the evening. I never paid this charge, nor did I engage in anything outside of the bar with them.

In Singapore, we went to one of two bars: The Wall and some little dive bar across the street from the Hard Rock Café. I have a picture of me and several friends drinking with two pitchers in our hands in the bar. One night, I drank so much that I had to find a friend of mine who was working Shore Patrol and ask him to get me a cab back to the pier. It was a rough night but a fun one.

The Wall was a different story. This was a bar that I went to on our second time in the port. It was a family-run bar. The owner was a local; his wife was from England. Their daughter worked in the bar as a waitress, and most of the younger guys from the ship were infatuated with her. She and I struck up several conversations, but I never hit on her. The bar began each night by showing Pink Floyd's The Wall on the televisions around the bar. They even sold T-shirts with the logo from the album. All the staff wore them. They sold out of these shirts frequently, and they were sold out during our week in port. This meant that no one could get them. By the end of the second night, I had a shirt, but not just any shirt. I had the shirt that the owner's daughter had been wearing that night. She finished her shift in a regular blouse while I walked out of there with her shirt in my bag. Several guys were jealous, and I was smiling all the way to the ship.

Our last port of call on the first cruise was Dubai. I do not like the heat, but I fell in love with the people and the architecture in Dubai. This was our first port where we could pull into a pier. We had a village of sorts set up on the pier with a bunch of food places in make-shift plywood buildings. As we left the ship, there were buses that would take us to the USO. From there, we could take a cab to the city. It was at the USO that I met a sheik. He invited me and a couple of the other guys to join him downtown for dinner. This was during Ramadan, when many Muslims would fast from sunrise to sunset.

When we got to the hotel downtown, he took us up to his meeting room. In that room, there were two long tables filled with food and drink. It was the biggest spread I had ever seen. He had serving girls and dancing girls in the room. Just like in Hong Kong, all of these were working girls, but I had no idea. This was our first night in port.

I did not drink a lot while in Dubai, mainly because it was Ramadan but also because they only had beer, which I do not like. But one night, a couple of guys I knew from the ship were drunk at the USO. We went outside to find a cab back to the ship, and the cabbies got into an argument over who would take us. The local police came running over, with sub-machine guns at the ready, and one of the drunk guys started asking the police if he could lie on the ground while the police pointed his gun at him, and his friend took a picture. This did not go over well with the police, who did not speak English.

While in Dubai, we had a shipmate pass away one evening while out for an evening jog. He was young, 36, and had a heart attack. After we left the port, they had a military Carrier

Onboard Delivery (COD) plane fly his remains out to us. We stored him in one of the freezers on the ship until we could transfer his remains to a supply ship, which then took his remains to be flown back to the United States. From here, we returned home via Singapore, Hong Kong, and Hawaii. I was expecting to be met on the pier by a couple of different women, but no one was there.

Our second cruise was vastly different. North Korea was acting up at this time. We spent about 2 months in port in Japan. We still got to go to Hong Kong, but most of our time was spent in Japan and Korea. We spent about a week in Seoul, Korea, in addition to Japan and Hong Kong. Oh, and I was married during this cruise. Japan was nice, not as nice as Dubai, and Korea was crowded. I had less fun on this cruise but still had some great times.

I spent 6, mostly wonderful years in the Navy. During that time, I had training in Great Lakes and Dam Neck. My first command was in San Diego. There, I was stationed on the USS Kitty Hawk. My next and final command was on the USS Abraham Lincoln in Washington state. I was discharged shortly after we moved our home port from Bremerton to Everett.

While I was stationed in San Diego, I met Debbie. I had gone home for the weekend and decided to see my friend, Jack. His parents and I had always been friendly with each other, so when I got there, they invited me out to dinner with them and a friend of Jack's. I found out later that Jack had made himself scarce that weekend because of Debbie coming over. He was ghosting her, and his parents saw an opportunity to turn her attention to me instead. It worked. We were married a couple of months later. Our marriage had more to do with her getting pregnant than anything else. We were married in November, and my parents attended the ceremony. My dad insisted that she have a sip of champagne despite being pregnant at the time. Our son was born in May the following year. It was a rough pregnancy, but both parties came through it, and I had an amazing son to love.

When I say that it was a rough pregnancy, I am not using this term lightly. Debbie and I were married before her marriage was finalized. She had been told early in life that she would probably need to have a C-section because her birth canal was too small. We were lucky that we were able to get an exception, which meant that she could see a civilian OBGYN. Her doctor was located on Coronado Island, where I was stationed. During the holiday season, we went up to Orange County to visit family. On our way back to San Diego, we were rear-ended on the freeway. It was a hit-and-run accident. During the impact, the back of Debbie's seat moved forward and then went all the way back. We waited for an ambulance because I was concerned about her and our son being injured in the accident. For whatever reason, probably because I was ranting like a madman, the ambulance crew decided to put me on a stretcher and have me looked at for possible whiplash at the hospital as well. All three of us were fine.

A few weeks before our son was born, I rushed Debbie to the hospital. We had a couple of sailors over to our house for a home-cooked meal, and while taking them back to the ship, Debbie became violently ill and vomited all over the inside of our car. We were both concerned that this was something more than just being sick and that it could have something to do with the pregnancy. We were wrong, and both she and the baby were fine.

Our son was born on the Monday following Mother's Day. We had the day scheduled because of concerns over natural childbirth. They brought Debbie in, induced labor, and broke her water for her after a few hours. During this, they gave her an epidural. Both Debbie and I freaked a little bit at the size of the needle used for this. It was 12 hours after they broke her water that they decided to perform the c-section. During this time, she had dilated to 3cm and then back to 1 cm. Once they had Debbie prepped, they began to make the first incision. It was at this point that Debbie screamed. The doctor asked her what was wrong. Debbie responded by telling them that she knew where they were cutting and could feel it. They upped the dosage of the anesthesia at this point.

I was at Debbie's head, holding her hand, during the delivery. She was a real trooper throughout. When the doctor announced that I had a son, I quickly looked over the barrier they had erected and regretted it. I could see where they had cut her open and, what looked like, poured iodine over her muscle tissue. But I had a son. The nurse quickly distracted me with my son and took me over so that they could get his measurements and tie off the umbilical cord. Once they had it tied off, they had me cut the remaining cord off. I had no idea it would be so hard to cut. By the time we were done, Debbie was gone from the room.

What I did not know was that she was fading fast, and they had to get her to ICU. I think that there may have been some internal bleeding involved, but the doctor and her team were able to stabilize Debbie. Our son was ready to go home later that day, but Debbie was kept for treatment and observation for an additional 3 days. It did not make it any easier that *Don't Take the Girl* was released earlier that year, and it was a song that both of us loved. It is still hard for me to listen to, as it brings the memories of my son's birth flooding back to me. Once I realized that Debbie was no longer in the room, I was frantic and fearful for her.

In January, before my son was born, I went through CPR Instructor training on the ship. I was the only non-medical personnel in the training, which many people thought was odd, but I loved it. My son was born in May, and 5 weeks later, we left for our second West Pac cruise. During that cruise, all of us who went through the class trained and qualified roughly 2500 people in CPR. It was intense, and it was fun. We returned to the States a couple of days before Christmas.

During the cruise, my wife and I had been approved to move into base housing. She did this by herself because of my absence. Money was tight at the time. We had no tree, no food, and no presents, but we had some awesome neighbors. Our next-door neighbors reached out to their church and surprised us with a tree right before Christmas. They also had some ornaments for us. Then they invited us over for dinner with them. Over the next year, we got to know them even better, along with several other families in the neighborhood. In August, I was up for reenlistment and new orders. Because of what was going on in the world, such as the Gulf War, orders would be delayed until the following year. I still reenlisted.

The next year, I called for my orders and picked Bremerton, Washington. I was going to remain on sea duty and was headed to another carrier, the USS Abraham Lincoln. We moved in May of that year. I found a nice little house for us in Tacoma and even had an old high school friend living not far away from it. By this time, Debbie was pregnant with our second child, a girl. Our daughter was born in August of that year. Our family was complete, but not for long.

The ship was in dry-dock, and crew moral was extremely low. Most of the unmarried personnel lived in BEQs on base, but many of them were put up in hotels in Tacoma. Oh, and the crew was co-ed. This was new to me and not what I had signed up for. This was the beginning of male and female integration on combatant vessels. It led to the men spending a lot of time, in close quarters, with females. Shortly after arriving at this command, I was transferred to the departmental office as office support. There was a female petty officer who had also been assigned this duty. She was single and would spend much of her free time on the ship in the office. This included nights that I was on duty. Our conversations became very casual, much more casual than I would engage in today.

During these casual conversations, comments would be made by both parties of an inappropriate nature. At some point, I made a very off-color comment, and she was worried that someone else may overhear it, so she reported me. I have no idea about her motivation in reporting me, nor do I care at this point in my life, but what I said was wrong and should have been reported. Because of her report, there was an accusation, and I went before a non-judicial punishment, Captain's Mast, where he recommended that I go before a review board for punishment. The board voted 2-1 to keep me in the Navy, but the captain had other plans. This was not long after the Tailhook scandal, so the Navy was cautious about these types of accusations. I was sentenced to a 30- or 60-day restriction, reduction in rank, and ½ months' pay forfeiture for the duration. In addition to this, I was administratively separated from the Navy. It broke my heart, but I deserved it. If I could go back and change what I did, I think I would.

Married Life – Post Service

Upon leaving the military, I went to work for a security firm. I started out as a mobile security supervisor. This meant that I would drive around to multiple sites, making sure that the buildings were locked up and that nothing was happening on site. If I received a call from someone at the property, I would respond to the site and clear everything up. It was an easy job, but I worked overnight – 2000 - 0600. This also meant that Debbie and I rarely saw each other. It was while working here that I met my second wife.

Nikki worked for another security company. They had an office at one of the buildings we patrolled. During the night, I would see her in the parking garage. We would talk and get to know each other. She was a divorced mother of two. Her ex lived in Las Vegas. She had moved to Washington because she was from here, and her mother still lived up here. I am not sure when it happened, but she and I came to be more than just friends. I was trying to make things work with my wife, and she with her ex. Eventually, we thought it would help if we could just release some of our sexual frustration with each other. That was one of the dumbest things I ever did.

Debbie and I separated in December, and I moved in with Nikki right away. That Christmas, after I moved in, I was barbecuing on the balcony at Nikki's condominium. Apparently, I freaked out the neighbors because they called the fire department. Once the firefighters showed up, I took them out to the balcony to show that I was simply grilling dinner for us. It was funny at the time, especially because it was snowing. Who grills in the snow? This guy!

Once Debbie found a place to live, she moved out of our apartment, and I moved back in with Nikki and her kids. We stayed there for another couple of years. When it came time to renew our lease, the management company denied us. They used some crazy reason for it, but the reality was that they were remodeling the buildings and grounds. This would allow them to charge more rent, but not as much as they could to new tenants. They had to get rid of the older residents when their leases were renewed. So, we moved in with Nikki's mom. After a few months of saving, Nikki and I bought our first home, a double-wide trailer in Renton.

We moved into our new home on November 1, 1999. It was in a nice area of Renton, down off Maple Valley Highway. It was close enough to the city that we could get there quickly, yet far enough away that we could enjoy the peace and quiet as well. I was working at Radio Shack as a store manager, and Nikki worked for the same security company. She would soon leave that company and go to work for an aerospace company where her grandmother used to work.

The following year, I would apply to that same company and go to work at a different location in Renton. Nikki made more money than I did, but I worked closer to home. It worked out well for us. In her role as an administrative assistant, though, she met many engineers in the company. It was one of those engineers who ultimately caught her eye. After a tumultuous time in our short marriage, Nikki left me to move in with this gentleman, whom she later married. Nikki moved out of our home and took almost everything in it. She left me the appliances and our bed. Other than that, anything that was ours together, she took. I was alone for a few months. I found a friend to rent a room from me, but I spent most of my time in chatrooms, bored. It was here that I met Jamie.

My regular modus operandi at this time was to go to work every day. I worked 0800 – 1630, roughly, and then returned home in the afternoon. I would typically make something easy; pepperoni quesadilla was a favorite, then fire up the old desktop and go hang out in yahoo chatrooms. It was while in one of these that I saw a moniker that reminded me of home. It was the popular nickname of a particular city I was familiar with, and "girl." We began chatting in the common room for several days, then took it to our private chat. Sure enough, this young lady was from the town, I thought. Her name was Jamie, and she was a divorced mother of three.

Over the next several days, we would chat regularly. I ended up sending her a cellphone on my plan line so that we could communicate via text and phone without giving her an expensive phone bill. Jamie lived in Orange County, and I was planning on heading down there for Thanksgiving, so we made plans to meet up. I got off work on Wednesday at noon. Debbie dropped the kids off with me at work, and my kids and I headed south as soon as I got off work. We stopped for about an hour in Sacramento so I could get some sleep in Denny's parking lot, but we arrived at my grandparents' house at about 1330m on Thanksgiving Day.

We were staying with my mom for the weekend. After taking my kids to her place, I went out for a drive to see some of the old neighborhoods. Jamie and I talked on the phone, and she asked me to stop by for a second, so I did. We already had plans to go on a date Friday night. She gave me her address, and I found her house. She met me in the yard. She did not want me to get out of my truck, so she came out to me. It was a wonderful experience, especially after so long. The next night, we met up and went to dinner. I forgot what else we did that night, but I ended up spending the weekend with her. We went to the zoo and had a party. I went home on Sunday.

Over the next few months, Jamie would fly up to Seattle to see me every other weekend. We spent a lot of time together and talked daily on the phone. For Christmas, because my kids would be with Debbie, I flew down to California and spent the holiday with her family. The next time I flew down there was the weekend before Valentine's Day. That was the weekend that her kids and she would be moving up to Washington and into my house. We loaded up her car with as much as we could and left early on the 14th of February. We stayed that night in Yreka, CA. The next day, we arrived back at my place.

That first Christmas together in Washington was when I should have seen what was going to come. Jamie spent about $2500 on presents for the kids. That is $500 per kid. It was a lot more than we could afford, but Jamie did a lot of her shopping in secret, with no one else around. This was our first major argument. After that, she toned down how much she had spent.

We were married the following year in a local park. My friend and former roommate, Cliff, performed the ceremony.

Washington has this interesting tidbit where anyone can perform their wedding ceremony, so long as the couple in question feels that this person can do so. Jamie was an atheist, and I was only marginally involved with Blue Moon and Caer Pugetia, so it was fine by me and saved us a lot of money. Blue Moon was a Wiccan training coven that I helped with, and the Bards of Caer Pugetia were a local druidic grove affiliated with the Order of Bards, Ovates, and Druids. Over the next few years, I would phase myself out of Blue Moon and become more ingrained with Caer Pugetia for a while. Ultimately, I would leave both entirely.

When Jamie and I met, she worked for an arm of a larger bank before transferring to the headquarters of the parent bank as a Vice President. Her position with the bank came with some benefits for us. We could watch the Macy's Thanksgiving Day parade from the comfort of her office rather than in the freezing cold and rain. It also allowed us to park, often for free, in Seattle so that we could go shopping or to shows. The bank was very good to us until it went under at the beginning of the housing market bust in 2008. I was still working for the aerospace company at this time.

In 2012, I decided to investigate Freemasonry. King Solomon Lodge in Auburn, Washington, had a weekly breakfast that I began to attend. This allowed me to get to know some of the guys and determine if this was a good lodge for me to join. I applied in March to receive the degree of Masonry. The way this happens is you need to ask a Mason to join. They can then give you a petition for the degrees. Once this is filled out and returned with the required fees, the Master of the Lodge will appoint a committee to meet with the candidate. They will then make their report to the Lodge. After the second reading of the petition, the Lodge members will then vote on the candidate. The vote is anonymous and consists of each member placing either a black ball or a white cube in the voting box. No one is supposed to know how another Mason votes.

The committee that met and asked me a lot of questions about my background. To be eligible for Masonry, you must be a male, 18 or 21 years old (depending on the rules of the Grand Lodge), and must have a belief in a higher power. In some jurisdictions, having a felony in your background may also disqualify you, but that depends on your Grand Lodge. During my investigation, when I met with the committee, one of the members focused on my belief in a higher power. He was a Christian and felt that if you were not a member of one of the three main religions, Christian, Jew, or Muslim, then you did not believe in a higher power. My first petition was rejected, presumably because I was not a Christian. This caught many of the Lodge members off guard as it had not happened in over a decade.

The Lodge Secretary reached out to me to let me know how the vote went. He was refunding me the fees and was very apologetic. I now had to wait for 12 months before I could apply again. This was not the first disappointment in my life and would not be the last.

I reapplied in April 2013 and was accepted in June of that year. I was initiated into the Degrees of Masonry on June 14th, passed to the Degree of Fellowcraft on February 24th, and then raised to the degree of Master Mason on May 19th. Between each of these, you need to prove your proficiency by memorizing a certain lecture, which includes being knowledgeable of the tools used in each ritual and of certain signs and words that are used to tell other Masons that you have achieved that degree. This is all done from memory. The last step, this proficiency, was made on December 8th. On December 13th, I was installed as the Senior Deacon in the Lodge.

Each Lodge has what is called the Line. These are the officers of the Lodge and those who are working their way through various stations in the Lodge. The primary officers of the Lodge are the Junior Warden, who sits in the South, the Senior Warden, who sits in the West, and the Worshipful Master of the Lodge, who sits in the East and runs the Lodge. Each position lasts for one year, after which you will typically move on to the next stations. These stations include the officers of the Lodge, the Junior and Senior Deacons, and the Junior and Senior Stewards. These seven stations make up the Line in a Masonic Lodge. In addition to these are the Secretary, Treasurer, Chaplain, Marshal, and Tyler. Each position has specific roles and responsibilities within the Lodge. I was also made a member of the Building Committee.

2014 – The Year That Everything Changed

The year 2014 is when my world came crashing down on me and the year in which I was reborn from the ashes. Jamie and I were having problems in our marriage. We had just come off the Christmas holiday season, and I asked that we spend it quietly at home, yet she insisted that we go to her parents' house like normal.

In February, I began a new position at work. I became the Health, Safety, Environmental, and Facilities Manager for our location. This position boosted me from an hourly employee to a salaried employee. This meant that I no longer earned overtime for more than 40 hours per week. The downside, at the time, meant that I would also be traveling. That travel took me out of Washington for a week every month. At first, I was not excited about this, but I quickly came to look forward to it. In fact, my first day in my new role was celebrated with me being in Phoenix for the week, right before my birthday.

I flew out Sunday afternoon, I think, and flew back on Friday. When I got home, things were as bad as ever. I flew out again the first week of March, and the thought of going home gave me anxiety. Not long after my return, Jamie and I sat down to talk about what I was feeling. I told her that I thought we should separate. She was not happy about it, but I packed my stuff and found a room to rent nearby so that we could continue to work on our marriage. But my heart was not in it.

I was still involved in Masonry at the time. This took up some of my free time, and Jamie and I would set up the occasional date. We would go to dinner and talk, and sometimes I would even spend the night with her, but I would always leave in the middle of the night or early in the morning before the kids woke up. I would also adjust my schedule to do things with the kids. Jamie did not want to file for divorce but asked me to do it, and quickly, so that she could move on with her life. I still love her and care deeply for her.

March 27, Easter Sunday, I found myself in a Nazarene Church in Renton. It was an interesting encounter, but not what I was looking for. See, in making the decision that Jamie and I could no longer continue as a married couple, at least not as the same couple we had been up to this point, I began looking for a deeper meaning to life. Wicca did not provide answers. Druidry did not provide answers. I thought that I might finally find those answers in Christianity, and I remembered that Nazarene Church I had briefly attended when I was a senior in high school.

After this disappointing encounter, I was not ready to call it quits, though. I conducted an internet search and found one in Federal Way. I decided to try that one. I was looking for a church where I felt comfortable and drawn. I had no idea how I would know, but I knew that I would know. On April 3rd, I went to the Federal Way Church of the Nazarene. I arrived early that day but did not want to interrupt whatever they had going on in the foyer before the service. I could see several people there, sitting around tables, with one guy at the front of the foyer instructing them. This was a familiar setting to me from my school days. During the sermon, the pastor focused on Romans 12:2, "Do not conform to the pattern of this world but be transformed by the renewing of your mind. Then you will be able to test and approve what God's will is – his good, pleasing and perfect will."

This caught my attention. After exchanging a few pleasantries, I left the service that day and immediately went out to purchase a Bible. I texted an old friend of mine, that same girl I had dated when I was attending Buena Park First in high school, and asked her if there was a particular translation I should get. I did not know much about the various translations at the time, and I thought that her insight would prove useful. She recommended the New International Version, NIV, so that is what I picked up. From there, I went back to my room and focused on reading Romans. I had no idea how to read the Bible at the time. Over the next several weeks, while laying in my rented room on a blow-up mattress, I found myself using my PlayStation to look for movies and stuff on the internet. Almost all of them ended up having Christian themes. The one that impacted me the most was *The Ride*. This was a short film about a taxi driver who decided to pick up one last fare before heading home. That last fare was a man who was on the verge of suicide. I had been there just a brief time before. The passenger is driven around by this taxi driver, as the driver pours into him and listens to his story. By the end of the film, the man decides to go home to his parents rather than kill himself. This film still holds a special place in my heart.

Week after week, I continued to attend that church on Sundays. Eventually, after a couple of weeks, I began to get to the church earlier and join their Sunday School class – that meeting in the foyer before the service. The pastor, Chuck, was still focused on Romans 12:2 and how we should put that into action daily. It is through our understanding of God, which is gained through the reading of the Word (Bible) that we begin to see the world through a biblical lens rather than through the lens of the modern culture. God will speak to us through His Word and through our interactions with other Christians. I knew that my old friend had been raised in the church, so we continued to talk, and she would share some aspects of her faith journey with me. Sadly, she shared other things with me. We began a relationship over the phone, which culminated in another level in May.

Our relationship was rocky, especially as I was trying to deal with my feelings about her and Jamie, dealing with being alone and missing my kids. I fell into a state of depression as I contemplated my life and the choices that had led me here. Just before Memorial Day, I found myself in my room, crying, with a gun in my mouth. I had no hope for a future. I did not yet know Jesus. I wanted to pull that trigger so badly because I was a coward. The only reason I did not pull the trigger was the thought of what my kids would go through when they found out how much of a coward their father was. I unloaded my firearm and got rid of it the next day.

In May, I went to South Carolina for a work meeting. Angela and I had made plans to meet up that following weekend. I flew out from Seattle on Sunday and then back on

Friday. Right after my return on Friday, I flew out to San Diego for the weekend. I took a shuttle to a hotel near the airport and then went for a walk and train ride to where Angela worked. We met up for dinner, and she took me back to my hotel to drop me off. We spent several hours talking and catching up. Prior to our meeting, Angela dropped a bit of a bombshell on me – she was pregnant. I knew this before I flew down there.

Now, Angela had told me that her boyfriend at the time, the father of her unborn child, was in and out of the picture. He was a man around her age who was dealing with his addictions. Angela was divorced twice and a single mom of two teenage girls at this point, with another coming in September. Her (ex)boyfriend had decided to go to truck driving school to further his career. After my return to Seattle, Angela and I continued to talk over the phone. I went down to visit her a few more times, including the first week of July.

In June, I moved into an apartment in Federal Way. I wanted to be close to the church I was attending and still within a reasonable drive to work. It did not hurt that it was also within 10 minutes of the Masonic Lodge I was a member of. Angela and I made plans for me to come down for a visit in the first week of July. I was going down there to help get her apartment ready for the new baby. This meant moving furniture, helping to get it cleaned up, and getting to know her two other daughters. This also meant that we would have an opportunity to take our relationship to the physical level, which we both wanted at the time. I thought that we would spend the 4th of July together, but it seems that she had other plans. You see, when we had dated in high school, I had hurt her very deeply. Deeply enough that all other men were measured against me as to how much of a jerk they were. No one had ever been a bigger jerk than me.

After talking with Angela about leaving, I had planned to leave on the evening of the 4th, which was a Friday. I fell asleep in the chair in her front room, where I had been sleeping all week, waiting for her to come home. I wanted to say goodbye to her before I left. I woke up early in the morning, said my goodbyes, and left at about 0500. A couple of hours later, I found myself in Los Angeles with a flat tire. I tried to change it, but apparently, the wheel had become rusted on the lugs and disc system. I had to call AAA to come out. It took them a while to get there, and he had to use a 4X4 and a hammer to break it loose. Once we got my spare on it, I continued my way to Barstow to get the tire replaced. It took about 3 hours to get it replaced, but I was back on my way after that.

The remainder of the drive through California and Oregon was mundane, with only one stop of note – the 45th Parallel in Oregon. I wanted to stop and take a picture of the road sign on Interstate 5. It was already late by the time I got there, and I was getting tired. I arrived back at my apartment around 0230, but I had no recollection of the last 30 miles or so. The last thing I remembered on that drive was hitting the southern outskirts of Olympia and then seeing Enchanted Village right before my exit. I took my bags upstairs, sent Angela a text to let her know that I had made it home safely, and then went to bed. A short time later, I woke up feeling fully refreshed. I remember thinking that I got to go to church that morning and being excited. I thought I might be late, but when I looked at my clock, it was only 0630, so I was on time.

That morning, we had visitors from Northwest Adult & Teen Challenge speaking at the church. I had never heard of this organization before. It is a program for young men who are dealing with drug and alcohol addiction. It is a difficult program to get into, and these men are given opportunities to improve themselves while fostering a relationship with Christ. During Sunday School, we heard from about three of these young men. Their stories were heart-wrenching, to say the least. Many of them had been in and out of trouble, many doing time in jail and juvenile hall, and all of them hit rock bottom when they lost everything, including their families. During the service, we heard from three more, including the director of the program. By the end of this, I was sobbing softly at the realization that I, too, was broken, just like all these men had been. I needed a savior, and Jesus Christ was that savior. After he told his story, he asked if there was anyone in the sanctuary who wanted to ask Jesus into their heart as Lord and Savior. I knew that I should, but I also knew how broken and horrible I was. He asked that everyone in the sanctuary bow their head and close their eyes. When he asked if anyone wanted to invite Jesus into their heart, he asked them to raise their hand. It was at this point that I felt a hand on my left shoulder and heard a comforting voice in my right ear say, "It is ok. It is time to come home." Do not ask me how, but I knew that it was the hand and voice of Jesus. No one in that sanctuary was closer than 10 feet to me. No one else could have touched me or whispered in my ear, and if they could, who would?

After asking for Jesus to be my Lord and Savior, I was weeping openly. Shortly after that, one of the members of the church came to pray for me. It was Scott, a man I would later consider to be a friend. Quickly, I was filled with a sense of peace and calm. I was also full of excitement. No one at the church acknowledged my newfound faith. I found out years later that this was because they all thought I was a longtime believer, and none of them realized that I had just had an encounter with the Living Christ.

I was so excited that I practically ran out of the church to my car. Once in my car, I called Angels to share the good news with her. She was excited for me. I could not get enough. I went back to my apartment, cracked open my Bible, and began to read from the beginning. On Sundays, I had made it a practice to prepare my dinner the night before, so all I had to do was turn on my little crockpot. My dinners were simple on Sundays, typically consisting of a small roast with some veggies and potatoes. I spent an enjoyable evening reading and eating a delicious dinner.

The following weeks at work continued much as they had, with little stress or turmoil. Jamie and I continued to talk regularly, as did Angela and me. But I still had a lot of time to myself, which was not good for me. I found myself spending more time in my head, especially at night and grew accustomed to getting little sleep. I was still learning about God and struggling with the flesh. This found me looking to Jamie for physical and emotional gratification, to Angela for emotional satisfaction, and to a new friend, Kelly, for physical comfort. I am ashamed of the life I was living at the time, trying to balance between two worlds, effectively trying to serve two masters.

In August, I received a message that Angela was heading to the hospital in labor. Her water had broken, and the baby was coming. I jumped on the next flight out to San Diego. I landed at the airport and was at the hospital within an hour of "our daughter" being born. Yes, I thought of this new baby as ours. I had been talking to her in the womb during my visits to California and had been making plans with Angela for her and all three girls to move up to Washington with me. I spent a week in San Diego with her and the baby. The baby's father? Well, he was in North Dakota with his ex-wife. He did not come home until after I left. I found out later that Angela had never told him about me and that he still believed that they were a couple.

Not knowing any of this, I still would fly down every month to visit. In October, I flew down for a visit and to attend training for my job. On October 5th, I became a member of the Federal Way Church of the Nazarene, even though I was not in attendance that day. In November, I found out about a position at the Torrance location and applied. It was not a sure thing, but I felt drawn to apply for it. Over the next few weeks, I had several rounds of interviews with members of the team there. My counterpart, Viktor, called me to ask why I had applied for a position that he felt was beneath me. At this company, salaried positions are broken into pay bands. Viktor held my same title there. He was a band-4 employee and thought I was the same at my location. I informed him that I was a band-3 employee due to the smaller size of my current location. This would be a lateral move for me and much more within my scope and desire for my career with the company. The year finished with me beginning conversations with my mother, who had fallen on some serious tough times down in California. With my ongoing relationship with Angela and my mom needing me to be closer to her, this job seemed like an answer to prayer.

I was raised to the sublime degree of a Master Mason on May 19, 2014. I proved my proficiency in this degree on December 8th, 2014, and was then installed as the Senior Deacon on December 12, 2014. Along with being installed as Senior Deacon, I was appointed to the Temple Association.

2015 – Learning to See God's Plan

In January 2015, I flew down for an in-person interview at the Torrance location. After the interview, before heading back to Washington, I met up with Angela in San Diego. It was then, in the parking lot of the mall, that Angela told me that she had gotten pregnant by her ex-boyfriend again and that she had had an abortion. She claimed that he had forced himself on her, and I was furious. She said that she had had an abortion because she could not ask me to raise another man's child again. What she did not know about me was that I had always been anti-abortion and would have loved that child as my own as well. I found out months later that she never believed that I could ever love our daughter as much as the man who was her biological father, who did not even want to be involved in her life. I was angry at him and disappointed in her.

A few days later, I received an offer for the position in Torrance and began to plan my move down. I also felt the need to be baptized before I left Washington. I could not explain it, but I began talking to Chuck about being baptized back in December. Chuck always put me off because I had been baptized as an infant, but then, in January, he decided to have a baptism at church. There were two of us getting baptized that day. It was January 25th, 2015. I was extremely nervous, but I knew it was what God was calling me to do. Tibe and I were baptized that day. I was moving two weeks later, yet in God's timing; I was baptized into the faith by a man I had come to love and call a friend.

Several people from the church came to help me load up my moving trailer. It was an interesting affair as I had a 2012 Dodge Charger with which I was pulling it. The trailer was so heavy that it brought the rear end of my Charger down so low that the car and trailer formed a bit of an angle when hooked up, about 165 degrees. I headed off to California. I wanted to be there before my birthday, and I made it to Buena Park on the 13th. After dropping my stuff off at a storage unit, I found a cheap hotel to stay at. On Valentine's Day, I went to San Diego to see a movie with Angela and have dinner. The movie we went to see was 50 Shades of Grey. If you know anything about this book, it should help you to understand how dysfunctional our relationship was. Both of us knew how tame these books were, as we both had experience with behaviors that go far beyond what these books portrayed.

I remembered that little church, Buena Park First Church of the Nazarene, from my youth. I began attending, hoping that I would find the same thing I had found in Washington. The pastor who had been there then had recently retired. They had a new, younger pastor leading the church. Doug was from the Oklahoma City area. He had just started on January 1st and seemed to have settled in quickly. I saw several people that I remembered from all those years ago, and they thought they knew me, although it turns out that they had me confused with someone else. Two weeks after arriving in Buena Park, I found a wonderful apartment complex with two bedrooms. The price was right, and it included many amenities. It was right across the street from the high school where I graduated.

I would spend every weekend driving to San Diego on Friday, getting a hotel for the weekend, and driving home either Saturday night or early Sunday morning. I always made sure that I was at church on Sunday mornings, even on those weekends when I stayed in San Diego until after church, which I did about once a month. When I stayed in San Diego until after church, I would attend a Pentecostal church that I could walk to from Angela's apartment. Angela never attended church with me, or at all for that matter.

As time went on, our relationship soured. Angela was focused on forcing the baby's father to be involved in her life. He was still drinking heavily and had even lost his job as a truck driver after suffering a heart attack in the cab. Thankfully, he was in a depot at the time, so no one was hurt. Angela, being his listed point of contact, was called to the terminal to clean out his truck while he was in the hospital. She found some things that were disgusting, yet she continued to stand by him.

At one point, Angela's oldest daughter was involved in a vehicle accident. She had been blinded by the sun at an intersection, did not see the other car or the traffic light, and the collision totaled the vehicle she was driving. They only had one car. I quickly offered to let Angela drive my car until she was able to get something to replace it. This surprised her. I knew that I could take a bus to work for about $15 each way and over two hours of transit time or get a ride from a coworker who lived not far from me. To me, it was no big deal as I was trying to help a friend. It seemed to be important to her because no one had ever done this for her before. I was trying to show her that I was quite different from that jerk when we were in high school.

That summer, my mom moved in with me. It had become apparent that Angela was never going to move in with me, which was the whole reason I had rented a 2-bedroom apartment, and my mom needed help as she was getting ready to have knee surgery. I began going to San Diego less often, maybe every other week, and had begun going on long walks on my days off and when I was home for the weekends. I would even take the bus to Disneyland, where I had bought season passes for all four of us, and then walk home after walking around the park. One day, I walked over 26 miles. I would also swing by Buena Park 1st on Mondays when they have something going on. Sometimes, it would be Monday Night Football. Other times, it would be a movie. Doug and I struck up a friendship during this time.

In August, I went to San Diego to help Angela with the baby's first birthday celebration. I knew that her biological father would be there, along with his family and Angela's. I tried to remain in the background as much as possible, but Angela's mother quickly recognized me from the past. She did not exactly warm up to me, but I did not get the cold shoulder I was expecting either. Angel's ex may have known about me, but he was too focused on trying to be the center of attention to do more than glare at me on occasion. The party went off mostly without a hitch.

September and October passed mostly without incident, but I could feel Angela growing distant. We would make plans, only for her to cancel them at the last minute. Many of these cancelations had to do with her desire to have her ex more involved in their daughter's life. I began to spend more time at home rather than going to San Diego. I had also begun praying for God to show me who He would have me spend the rest of my life with. In the meantime, it was getting harder and harder to spend time with Angela. We even went to a summer concert in San Diego. It was here that she told me that she would never get married again, which meant that our dating was pointless. If it was not leading to a God-ordained marriage, there was no point in pursuing it any further. Still, I had hoped to change her mind, and there was the baby I loved to consider.

As the holiday season got closer, things grew increasingly stressful. Right before Christmas, after an argument where I ended up leaving with a lot of things unsaid between us, I received an email from Angela. In her email, she essentially broke up with me after writing that she did not think I would ever care as much about her kids as their fathers. The problem was that neither of their fathers, Angela's first husband and ex-boyfriend, had any real desire to be a parent to their respective kids. A lot of it was a misunderstanding on my side, I am sure, but God had made it clear to me that this was not the relationship He had planned for me. It was in late December that I met this cute girl on a dating app, Natalie.

2016 – The Year of Change

Natalie and I met through E-Harmony. This was a supposed Christian dating site. I say supposed because most of the women I matched with were scammers located on Guana or those who were actively engaging in non-Christian behaviors. More than a few wanted to hook up, which was NOT what I was looking for at the time. Angela and I still talked. Some days, she acted like we were still a couple and other days, she acted like I was the biggest jerk in the world who would not leave her alone. I would actively talk to Angela because I love her daughter as my own, but I tried to guard myself from being taken in by her. I went on a few dates with other women, but none of them clicked. Natalie and I were exchanging email messages through the app. Eventually, we figured out a way to give her my phone number so that we could communicate directly if she was interested.

Natalie lived in the Valley, just above Los Angeles. It was not that far, but LA traffic was horrible. We began texting at the end of January or the beginning of February. Apparently, she had a pre-paid phone with limited text messages. She ended up calling me on the phone around my birthday. She got upset with me that I had not mentioned that it was my birthday, but this was the first time we had ever spoken on the phone. Why would I tell her before this? Anyway, her talking to me on the phone was one of the best and most unexpected things that happened in my life. We talked on the phone for a couple of weeks. I was still going on occasional dates with Angela and others at this point.

On March 5th, I had plans to meet one of these women at Disneyland – my pass was good until July. This was another lady I had met through E-Harmony. On Friday, the excuses began with her. She was telling me about a lot of drama with her ex, and then her ex got my phone number and started texting me. He was telling me that he had slept with her the night before and trying to tell me very personal things about her. I reached out to her directly about this. She gave me a story of how he was lying, and how we could still meet up. So, on Saturday, I went to Disneyland. While I was there, she kept texting me excuses for why she was running late and how she needed money for various things, and eventually, she just stopped responding. During this time, I texted Natalie to see how her day was and with my ex-wife, Jamie, just to talk. Jamie and I had gotten to a point where we could be friendly with each other. Strong emotions were still there, but it was somewhere between friendship and relationship. I jokingly told Jamie that I got stood up and then asked her if she thought I could find another date. She said that she knew I could set up another date and told me to ask out the "other girl" I was texting, Natalie.

I asked Natalie via text if she wanted to have dinner with me. She told me that she had to work and what time she got off. I told her great that I would drive up to her and then asked her if there was any special place she wanted to go for dinner. She gave me the name of a restaurant, and we decided to meet up around 1930 after she got off work. So, I left Disneyland, went home, and changed, and then began the long drive to meet this young lady. When I got to the restaurant, I found a parking spot close enough that I could see the entrance but not so close as to be conspicuous. There were several empty places around me. While I sat in my car waiting for her, I was about 30 minutes early, I noticed a car pulled into the lot and chose a spot just a few away from me. I began to chuckle to myself and think how funny it would be if that was Natalie pulling in. It was. We both got out of our cars and proceeded to meet each other. Then, we went in to get a table. It was extremely loud and crowded in the restaurant, so we ate our dinners and then went out to walk around in the cool air and talk.

We must have walked around that parking lot for an hour. Then we decided that we would go across the street to a Starbucks that was still open for something warm to drink. The parking lot in this shopping center was much bigger, so we began to walk around that one, too. After a few laps, I asked Natalie if it would be ok if I held her hand, as I did not want to be presumptuous. She thanked me for asking and agreed to let me hold her hand as we walked. After a few more laps, before we finished for the evening, I asked her if it would be ok if I kissed her. Again, she agreed. I was happy to kiss her.

During our revolutions around these two parking lots, our discussion focused mainly on God and who He was to each of us. I made it clear that I was not interested in dating for sport and had to know that there was at least the potential for something more down the line. Natalie felt the same way. Because of this, our questions were not the typical first date variety. Rather than asking superficial questions, favorite author, book, musician, movie, etc., we focused on what our respective faith journeys looked like. She told me about teaching in private education and traveling abroad as a missionary teacher. I told her about my journey to faith and what God wanted for my life. My career was going well; I had hopes of finding a position with the company that would involve a lot of travel, about 75%, and would take me all over the world. Natalie was interested in this. Before we went our separate ways for the evening, we had agreed to meet up for lunch the next day. Again, I would travel to meet her rather than ask her to come down to me.

On the drive home, we talked on the phone. She was only about 49 miles away, but in LA traffic, it took over two hours to drive it, and this was late at night. I got home a little after 0100. I went in and went to bed. The next morning, I drove to church instead of walking and then left to meet Natalie at her church, Discovery Church in Simi Valley. Discovery was a multi-service church, so I got there before the last service ended. Natalie was working in the bookstore at the church. After service, I followed Natalie to a park not far away. We laid out a blanket and had a wonderful lunch. More "not first date" questions ensued. I wanted to make sure that Natalie was open to the idea of marriage if the right person came along. She was, and in answer to one of my questions, she assured me that it would be a white wedding. She was not opposed to having kids, but it was not a lifelong dream for her either. After lunch, we went for a walk through the hills. I was not prepared for this. I had worn my cowboy boots, so the walk did not last long, but we had fun. I left her at about 1930 that evening because I had to work in the morning.

Monday and Tuesday, I went to work. Natalie and I would text during the day and talk on the phone at night. Wednesday, she asked if I wanted to come over to where she was staying. She was house sitting for her brother and his family. While there, we continued to talk. It was at this point that I learned how close I had come to not getting that first date. Natalie had been on the verge of chickening out, and her sister-in-law, Fay, made a snide comment, asking if Natalie had even dated this century. Fay finally convinced Natalie to go on the date, and I am glad she did. When Natalie asked Fay if it was okay if I came over after work, Fay happily agreed and then told Natalie where to find condoms in their house. She assured her that we would not need them, and we did not.

Natalie and I had a big laugh over this. I told her I had the perfect way to freak her family out. I had a ring in my car that I had bought several months ago. We should put that ring on her hand and then take a selfie of us, making sure that the ring was visible but not too visible. She could then send that picture to Fay, and we could laugh when she noticed it. Natalie agreed, so I went out to retrieve the ring. Now, in my prayers to God about helping me notice the one He picked for me, I asked Him to make it obvious because I could be dense. Well, when I put that ring on her hand, it would not come off. Message received by God, loud and clear. It was at this point that I became convinced that Natalie and I would be married soon. Natalie thought I was joking until I explained it to her. At this point, she was not happy with God, but she did not kick me out. I stayed the night, sleeping on the couch, and then went to work the next morning. I worked about halfway between our two residences.

Natalie and I began seeing each other every weekend, in addition to texting and calling each other daily. At first, her plan was to come down to see me, her best friend who lived a couple of miles away from me, who Natalie would stay with on the weekends. Natalie was off on Fridays but worked for a couple of hours on Saturdays. So, she would come down on Thursday night after work and go back Saturday morning before work. This quickly became her staying at my apartment. She did this because my mom lived with me, so we were not alone in my apartment. She soon turned over her duties at the bookstore to someone else; this way, we could go to church together.

At this time, I was attending Orangethorpe United Methodist Church at 0830 and then heading over to Buena Park First for their 1030 service. After Church, we would either go to the mall for a movie or just to walk around, or we would go to Knott's Berry Farm, where I had purchased season passes for the two of us. Both of us enjoyed people-watching and just walking around. It allowed both of us to spend time with each other and to continue to get to know each other. We began talking about getting married, and we both wanted to do it right. This meant that I wanted to ask her parents' permission to marry their daughter. There were a couple of problems with this: her parents were in Jericho, and with us living over an hour apart, it would be difficult for us to go through pre-marital counseling together. Memorial Day weekend, Natalie moved in with me.

I was finally able to tell her father my intentions with his daughter during a phone call with him. This caught him off guard because we had just started dating a few weeks earlier. It was around this time that I finally got to meet her brother, David and Fay. They decided to grill me on my intentions with Natalie. I politely listened to their accusations and assumptions and tried to calmly answer their questions. Neither of them liked before or after this encounter. Neither Natalie nor I let this concern us. We continued with trying to make plans for a wedding, the first aspect of which was to decide on a date. October was a hard month for both of us. My father passed away in October, and her grandma did the same. We knew it would be October, but the date was still in question. Natalie's sister, Rita, wanted us to get married on her birthday, not sure why, but I firmly removed that date as a possibility. Our wedding was going to be an event to celebrate Natalie, and she would not be sharing the limelight with anyone else. We eventually decided on October 1, 2016. October 1 was my father's birthday, and we felt it was a clever way to include him in our wedding. He had died 20 years earlier.

This was leading us into the summer. In June, Natalie's parents came back to the States to "take care of issues with the family home." The family home was where David and his family lived while her parents were in Jericho. Apparently, there was some paperwork that they needed to sign, and they had to be in California when they did it. It was an excuse to meet me and to let me know what they really thought about me. They had already heard how horrible I was from David and had made up their minds about me. When her parents flew in, the whole family went to lunch together, including Natalie and me. It was at that lunch that Cecelia, Natalie's mom, broke down and said a few things. First, she accused Natalie of no longer having a relationship with Jesus because she was getting married to me. The next was when she said, "I don't want you to make the same mistake as me," because I was divorced and had kids like Natalie's dad, Gene. Gene looked at his wife with shock on his face and said, "I'm sitting right here." Natalie and I laugh about this now, but it was a tense moment. Gene, ever the peacemaker, tried to calm things down. He said, "We love our daughter. We trust our daughter. If she likes you, we like you. We will like you a lot more if you are still around in a few years." I remember this and tease them about if they like me more now. Her parents were only around for a couple of days, and that was the only time Natalie got to spend with them on that trip.

Right around the 4th of July, Gene and Cecelia flew back into the US. They had to sign more paperwork for the house, but they became stranded in the US this time. Their plan for our wedding had always been to fly in the day before and then leave either right after the wedding or the following day. The thing is, they need to buy roundtrip tickets from the States each time. Seemingly overnight, the price of those tickets had tripled, which meant that they were stuck until the prices came down. Over the next few months, Natalie and her bridesmaids began planning for our wedding. This meant that Cecelia was around to be a part of it, which was an answer to Natalie's prayers. They planned dress fittings and bachelorette parties, and Natalie made sure to invite Cecelia to all of them.

We were more entrenched at Orangethorpe United Methodist than at Buena Park First. There are many reasons for this, but those are not germane to the discussion. We asked pastor John to do our premarital counseling. Both of us thought this was a crucial step for us, and John agreed. John knew some of my stories, my being divorced three times, and a bit of my pagan background, which is why he spent most of the time during premarital counseling trying to convince Natalie not to marry me. The problem is that she and I had already discussed all of this. We both shared our baggage with each other and worked through the implications. Nevertheless, he tried.

Now, when we got engaged, I made two promises to Natalie: that we would not get married in Las Vegas and that she would be a virgin on our wedding night. Natalie did not want to get married in Las Vegas because David and Fay had done that. From what I understand, it was not a classy affair. In fact, they told the rest of the family to meet them somewhere else, and then they ran off to Vegas to get married. When the family saw them next, they were married. Natalie wanted her wedding to be classy but wanted to make sure that those who showed up for the wedding were there to support us, not simply to see her parents. If we got married in California, we ran the risk of having the guest list explode as many people would want to come just to see her parents. It was stressful as we tried to figure this out. Eventually, Natalie relented to getting married in Las Vegas.

I began looking around at some of the wedding chapels in Vegas. Las Vegas is the wedding headquarters of the US. What had started as a novelty industry, weddings performed by Elvis had grown into a multi-billion-dollar industry. I found the Chapel of the Flowers and showed Natalie the website. It was tasteful and simple, just how Natalie wanted it. We called them and began to put everything into place. Our wedding date was available, so we picked a time slot and began planning for the event. The venue took care of almost everything for us. All we had to do was show up early to get our marriage license. The venue provided a limo to pick up the bridal party, photographers, and videographers to capture the event, and best of all – a limited number of people who could attend. We were limited to 20 people, plus Natalie and me. It was perfect.

At this point, I was working in aerospace, and Natalie was working as a tutor with a company. My company, in fact, the entire aerospace industry, had fallen into a significant downturn. This happens every few years, so many of us were not surprised. In 2015, I had a 1-week furlough from work. It made finances tough but not insurmountable. In July of 2016, we had a second furlough. I had already begun looking around for another job by that time. My job search took me to the East Coast a few times. None of them panned out, but I did not stop looking. In August, Natalie's parents approached her about what it would take for her to be able to focus on the wedding planning. They surprised us by offering her enough money to quit her job and pay for our wedding. This did not come out of nowhere, though. During one of the bachelorette parties, I went to pick up Gene and Cecelia from their hotel and then drove them to where everyone was meeting up to go to the venue for the party. During that drive, Cecelia lamented how she felt like a fifth wheel and that Natalie was only inviting her because she was stuck in the States. I almost slammed on my breaks at this point. I informed Cecelia that Natalie felt conflicted because she wanted Cecelia to be part of these events but that she also knew that her mother hated being in the States. Natalie felt that God had answered her prayers by keeping her mother here and that her mother would hate her if she knew. It was at this point I believe that Cecelia and Gene figured out that I not only love their daughter, but that I also listen to her. This caused a major change in our relationship, which I believe led to them offering a way for Natalie to focus on the wedding planning.

With our wedding date set for October 1st, I went ahead and requested time off from work so that I could go out early and receive people as they flew in. I was planning to take the week before and the week after off for our wedding and honeymoon. Then came the news that our company would have another furlough at this time. I would either need to take the furlough 2 weeks before our wedding or the week before our wedding. If I had taken it two weeks before, I would have needed to work the week before our wedding. I ended up taking that week before as my furlough week. I had also planned to head out to Vegas on Friday morning, but then my daughter wanted to come in on Thursday morning, so I headed to Vegas on Wednesday. This is where part of the nightmare begins.

I had originally booked a room at the Excalibur resort for Friday - Sunday. This would give us Saturday night in the bridal suite together. I needed to find a room for the extra two days. The room I already had at the Excalibur was booked until

Friday, and it was not exactly inexpensive. So, I looked for another hotel close to where we were going to be. I found the Hooters Resort. The price was right, so I booked the room. It was after this that I decided to look up Yelps reviews for the property. That was a major mistake on my part. I both enjoyed and was horrified at reading the reviews. The reviews talked about the tacky décor; what else would you expect from Hooters? But they also talked about how dated and disgusting many of the rooms were. Some of them alluded to working girls having their heads put through the wall during the course of their employment, and then the walls being covered with a bolt-on headboard, and the fear of patrons using blacklights in the room and seeing how much DNA was all over everything. Pretty scary stuff to read right before you head there for a few days.

My daughter and her boyfriend flew in on Thursday. They had wanted a couple of days to themselves in Vegas before the wedding. I picked them up at the airport and took them to In-N-Out for lunch. It was one of our favorite fast-food places to eat when we went to California. After that, we went back to my room until I could check them in at their hotel for the weekend. I do not think I saw them again until the wedding. On Friday, Natalie and the rest of the guests began to arrive. Natalie had an entire circuit she ran in California before coming out to Vegas. She went to pick up friends of hers, who had flown in from Moscow, along with several other friends who lived in California. She came out, and we met up in Vegas for dinner in the room where my mom and some of the other guests were staying. That same night, her other brother, Daniel, had said he wanted to take me out for a bachelor party. I am not one who generally enjoys going to clubs or bars, but I wanted to be polite, so I agreed. I went back to my room at the Excalibur and waited for Daniel to call. He never did. I ended up cracking open my window and listening to the Route 91 Concert going on across the street.

The next day was the wedding. I wore a black suit with a purple boutonniere. The boutonniere and bridal bouquet were designed and made by Denise, one of Natalie's bridesmaids and dear friend. I got to the chapel early and waited nervously for Natalie to show up. Once she arrived, they ushered us both off to sign some paperwork and then whisked Natalie away to get ready for the wedding. Our wedding was attended by my daughter and her boyfriend, my mother, and several members of Natalie's family. The wedding was also streamed online, so those who were not in attendance could watch it. I then took my place in the chapel; my daughter and Daniel were on my side. I caught my breath when Natalie entered the chapel. She was so beautiful. She was escorted by her father, who then gave her to me. The pastor began the service with a prayer. Natalie did not remember the prayer until we watched it later. She said that she was nervous I would bolt and leave her at the altar. Following the service, Natalie and I had a few more documents to sign and then the photo shoot. They took us outside to take pictures. They did large group shots, small group shots, and even shots of just Natalie and me. All the photos were tasteful and classy.

After the wedding, we had planned to have a reception lunch at the buffet at the Excalibur. Not many of our guests joined us, though. Rita had rented an air b-n-b for the weekend and had invited everyone except Natalie and me over for a barbecue. Almost all of Natalie's family decided to go to that. Only her parents and nephew came with us from her family. We only found out about the barbecue because her nephew said that he and his girlfriend were heading over there next. Yes, that is how petty her sister is. Rita has never forgiven me for putting her in her place when it came to the date of our wedding. But Natalie and I had fun with those who attended. Then we went back to our room to change before heading out to the Strip.

Sunday, we met up with my daughter and her boyfriend and then headed over to Hoover Dam. We had planned to take the tour, but the cast was astronomical. They were $30 per person plus the $10 we paid for parking. It would have been $130 for the four of us just to park and take a 1-hour tour. Instead, we walked out across the dam, which was all Natalie and Brenwynn wanted to do anyway. It was windy. I almost lost my hat a few times. When we looked over the dry side of the dam, I remember thinking how much fun it would be to slide down that thing. We spent the afternoon together before taking the kids back to their hotel room. Natalie and I went to the Tournament of Kings for dinner.

Monday morning, Natalie and I woke up, got dressed, and checked out of the Excalibur. That afternoon, we were meeting her parents at the chapel to decide which picture package we wanted from our wedding and to pick out the pictures we wanted to have included. We had several of the pictures on a thumb drive and ordered a couple of print photos. These now have a prominent place on our wall, including a metal picture of us inside the chapel. After deciding on the photos, we said our goodbyes to her parents; they were flying out to LA that day and would head back to Jericho before we returned to California. After this, Natalie and I went to check in at the resort where we would spend our honeymoon and our last week in Vegas.

The resort was ok. It was a time-share resort that I found on Facebook for $100. This gave us 4-nights and 5-days at the resort, so long as we sat through a 90-minute sales pitch for the time-share. We got checked in, went to our room, and unpacked. Natalie and I had decided to stay in for the evening as we were exhausted from dealing with family for the last three days. The room was nice, but we did have to call the concierge upon our arrival because something was not working in our room. Minor inconvenience. The rest of the week we spent taking the shuttle to the Strip, walking around, and people-watching. While on the Strip, we would sign up for the various time-share seminars in exchange for tickets to shows and meals. One of the shows we went to was a Zombie Burlesque show. It was a lot of fun for both of us. Thursday, we had our seminar for the time-share. Once the salesman found out that we had been at the resort all week, he lost interest in trying to convince us to buy. Yes, the resort was that bad.

When Friday came, it was time for us to head home. While loading up the car, I noticed a large dent in my car that had not been there previously. It was at the right height to be from one of their shuttle buses. We reported the incident to the management and asked to see the videos of the garage and the loading zone. Their head of security refused to show us the video, claiming privacy issues, so we reported the issue to LVPD. After filing our report, we hit the highway back to California. About an hour outside of Vegas, the head of security called us and told us that none of their cameras had picked up my car. I told him I found this difficult to believe as there were six cameras in the parking garage where I parked and three more at the spot where I was loading the car. Not a resort I would recommend after this. During the trip back, we stopped off at several roadside attractions, including the Thing and an alien attraction.

During the summer, I began looking for a new job. I found some stuff at my work that put me in an ethical bind. I found out that someone in the company, well above my pay grade, had figured out a way to continue to produce certain products and then ship them virtually so that we could continue to charge the government for them. This was not behavior that I could be involved with, and because of my position with the company, I would be guilty of this moral breach by association. My job search had taken me primarily to the East Coast. Natalie and I had no desire to remain in California, and there was not much keeping us there. I had promised Natalie that I would not field any calls related to the job search once our honeymoon began. I did have one iron in the fire, though. After talking to Natalie, I told them that I would be available Wednesday through Friday for a phone call about the position. They called, and we scheduled a trip for me to their location the week after our honeymoon.

Natalie and I got back to Buena Park late Friday afternoon. The next day, we woke up to a pleasant surprise – a wedding gift on our porch. We had several presents to open, including this one. Inside this package was a set of dishes that Natalie had asked for. She was overjoyed by this gift, but I think that the most special one, up to this point, was the gift received from her friend in Russia. Ruzanna and her husband had carried their present with them from Moscow. In there were some beautiful crystal champagne flutes. Natalie was excited that her friends could come all the way from Moscow, but giving her this gift made it even more special. We also received a gift from Natalie's former church – a 2-night stay at a hotel near Disneyland and a 2-day pass for Disneyland. This was Natalie's favorite place to go, so she was extremely excited about this. We planned to spend those 2-days at Disney in November. In the meantime, I flew off to my job interview on October 16th. The interview was on the 17th, and then I flew back on the 18th. It was with a major door manufacturer in Wisconsin. They decided to go with a local candidate, which was fine with me. I knew that God had someplace special for us.

November came, and we had two glorious days at Disneyland. The first day was all Disney, and the second was spent at California Adventures. We had a wonderful time. The biggest downside was that we both spent a lot of time scrolling social media on our phones while waiting in line for rides. Social media has this annoying knack for showing you things that you have talked about while your phone is around. Some people believe that your phone is always listening to you in order to show you these ads. The ads that kept popping up in my feed were for various seminaries and degree programs. I pointed this out to Natalie, who did not find it as humorous as I did. This was the beginning of my feeling that God was calling me into full-time ministry.

Up until this point, I had focused my job search on the East Coast. I talked to Natalie about her thoughts on me looking back in Washington. She told me to go ahead and look, and that we would talk long and hard before accepting anything there. I began looking and applying. Two jobs looked like they would be a good fit for me: Bellmont Cabinets and Tempur Sealy. I went through a few rounds of phone interviews with both, and then Bellmont decided to fly me up to Washington the week of Thanksgiving. I reached out to Sealy to let them know when I would be up there, and they asked if I could also come in a day early to interview them. I agreed and flew up on Monday, November 21st. I had an interview with Sealy on the 22nd and then with Bellmont on the 23rd.

Both interviews went well, but I was really impressed with Bellmont. Upon my arrival, I was escorted upstairs. In the stairwell was a framed certificate of appreciation from Billy Graham Ministries for the support and donations to their ministry. I also learned during the interview that the companys owner took several employees to Haiti every year. The employees would pay for their airfare, and the company would pay for everything else, including their hours of work. I learned about the history of this family-owned business and began to feel that this was where God was calling me. I left there after an hour and went to the airport to wait for my return flight to

California. Keep in mind that this was the day before Thanksgiving. About an hour before my flight, I received a call from the HR manager. She made me a verbal offer over the phone. I asked her if I could talk with my wife and pray about it over the weekend and that I would give her my decision by Monday. She agreed, and then I called Natalie to tell her about it.

Natalie and I prayed about it over the weekend and discussed it many times. That Sunday, Natalie and I decided to accept the position. I went to work that Monday and resigned. That resignation was supposed to be effective December 8th, but the company terminated me on the 7th. I was not fully prepared for that as I lost electronic access, which I discovered the morning of the 7th when I was trying to log into my computer. I went upstairs to talk with my friend in HR, and she was able to figure this out. That simply meant that I got to turn everything in and head back home much earlier than expected. I went home, and we loaded up my car to drive to Washington and find a place to live.

We took two days to get to Washington, arriving on Saturday afternoon. We stopped along the way and introduced Natalie to the wonder of stuffed hashbrowns from Sheri's. Natalie was hooked at the first bite. After that, we made a brief pit stop at Cabela's; we arrived at Don B's house. Don was a friend of mine with whom I used to work before I moved to California. Don was nice enough to let us stay at his house while we tried to find a new apartment. Because we made it to Washington on Saturday afternoon, Natalie and I decided to attend the *Installation of Officers* at my old lodge, King Solomon

#60. It was a fun night catching up with my Masonic Brothers and getting some pictures of Natalie and me.

The next day, we attended church somewhere and began our search for an apartment. I guess Natalie did not want to live in any city I had previously lived in, did not want the ghosts of my past. Knowing that I was going to be working in Sumner, we started off by looking in Pierce and South King counties. We drove out toward Buckley, but Natalie did not want to try and make that hill in the ice and snow. We tried a place in Federal Way, but they did not have an apartment to show us. They were willing to take our money though to apply. We passed. After this, we moved on to Auburn. The apartments seemed nice, and the rent was affordable. It was a definite maybe.

Our next stop was The Outlook in Puyallup. These were nice. They said that they were apartments, but they were more like townhomes. The garage was on the ground floor, along with a spare room. They said that many of their residents would use this as a storage room, but I thought it would be perfect for my mom. The middle floor had living areas, and there were three bedrooms on the top floor. The stairs would be a problem for my mom, but Natalie and I loved it. We went ahead and filled out the application and paid another non-refundable application fee. We left and went to get something to eat while we waited to hear back from the two apartments we had applied for.

The Outlook Apartments reached out first. They said that there was a problem with our credit checks and gave us a number to call. We called them and spent the next several hours trying to get the issue fixed, only to find out the next day that the issue was that Natalie had no credit history for them to look at, so they denied us despite my salary being more than enough to pay for the apartment. On Thursday, the 15th, we went and paid our deposit and 1st month for the apartment at Emerald Glen. We then went back to Don's to get our stuff and move into the apartment. We also stopped to pick up an inflatable mattress, a small television, and an electric griddle so we could cook. The good news was we now have a place to live. The bad news was that we did not have enough money to go back to California, get our stuff, and get back to Washington. A couple of days later, God would fix part of that.

Over the weekend, my former company made a direct deposit to my account. This was enough money for me to buy two last-minute, one-way fares from Seattle to Long Beach. We left Washington Tuesday afternoon. My mom came to pick us up and take us home. With my car in Washington, that meant that we still needed to rent a moving van, load up a two-bedroom apartment, and drive back up to Washington in winter. Well, on Wednesday, another check was deposited into my account, which was enough to rent the moving truck and get the three of us up to Washington. Natalie had always believed that God would have us somewhere new before Christmas. This was cutting it close.

We picked up the moving van on Thursday. Natalie's friend Denise and her son came to help us load the truck. That morning, it decided to start raining heavily. It was an absolute downpour, according to Washington standards, let alone California standards. I started loading up the truck while

Natalie and Denise packed up the apartment. After a few hours, Natalie discovered that my mom had not packed anything during the two weeks we were in Washington and had not packed anything yet either. This infuriated Natalie, but she and Denise got my mom packed. It also meant that I had to either unload the truck to fit my mother's stuff in there or leave a lot of my stuff behind when we left. Because of the rain, I decided that I would leave things behind. I left my barbecue, golf clubs, and some sentimental items behind. I was not happy.

Thursday night, I got us a couple of rooms at a local hotel. The plan was that they would head north while I went back to the apartment to do the final walk-through with the property manager. Our rooms were right across the hall from each other. While Natalie was taking a shower, my mom called me over to help her with something. I had just gotten undressed, so I quickly threw my sweatpants and a T-shirt on, leaving the clothes I had taken off piled up on the floor. While I was gone, Natalie came out of the shower. She saw my clothes piled up on the floor and saw my cell phone and keys on the table in the room and immediately had a panic attack. One of Natalie's greatest fears was that the Rapture would happen and she would be left behind. A few moments later, I came back into the room and found my wife almost in tears. I think it is hilarious, but Natalie is less enthusiastic about the memory of this event.

The next morning, Mom and Natalie headed north while I went back to the apartment. I was done much sooner than expected, so I was less than an hour behind the girls. We made it over the Grapevine about an hour before it was closed due to a snowstorm. The weather up north looked just as bad, so we took a detour to the before we got too far north. We spent the night on the coast and then headed up to Oregon the next morning. Before packing it in for the night, I told my mom that we wanted to leave at 0600. My mom was unresponsive the next morning. We called her cell and her room and even banged on her door. We finally called the manager to come and open her door. My mom finally answered her door around 0645. I guess she had turned the volume off on her phone and removed her hearing aids. I was not happy with her, but we finally got back on the road around 0800. Our path took us up through the southwestern section of Oregon, along the Pacific Coast Highway. Eventually, we turned east to reconnect with Interstate 5. We had made it around the nasty weather along the California/Oregon border. We pulled into the parking lot of our apartment at 2355 Christmas Eve. God had us in a new place before Christmas Day.

On Christmas Day, Sunday, we went to Federal Way Church of the Nazarene. It was a place I was familiar with, people I was familiar with, and a homecoming of sorts for me. The upside was that I knew many people there. The downside was that I knew many people there. When I left, I was dating a person who had just had a baby, and now I return two years later with a new wife. They, rightly so, believed that these two women would be one and the same and asked where the baby was. It took a few minutes to explain. Thankfully, because Christmas was on a Sunday, pastor Chuck had planned to have a candlelight service on Christmas Day. That was all that

Natalie wanted, and God did not disappoint her. Natalie and I talked about what kinds of churches we wanted to visit. Federal Way was not a guarantee for us as a family church. Natalie wanted to make sure it was where we both felt called, so, at the beginning of 2017, we shopped around for a church.

On the 26th, I made arrangements for 12th Man Movers to come over and help us unload the truck. It was a minimum 2-hour service, but the guys were done in about an hour. They were awesome. This gave us most of the afternoon to finish unpacking our boxes and bags before I had to get ready for my first day of work. That first day at Bellmont was exciting. I met my coworkers, a few of whom were also from California, and my teams. I had a great crew and began to learn a lot about the cabinet business. Luckily, this was also the end of the year, which meant that we were slow, and a lot of grace was given to everyone as we all struggled with the excitement of going home to be with family for the holidays.

2017 – The Journey Begins

Our apartment was in Auburn, my Masonic Lodge was in Auburn, and I worked in Sumner. This was a small 8-mile area for me to worry about. Now, we had to find a church. We checked out a few, but ultimately, we ended up at Federal Way Nazarene by the end of the month. Natalie and I enjoyed the church and many of the people. Mark M. was leading the Sunday School, and he was going through the Book of Revelation. When we first arrived, the class mainly sat there in silence, listening to what Mark had to say. He was trying to get them to join in the conversation, but it was almost as if they were afraid to say something. Here I come, speaking freely about my thoughts on the subject, even when they differ from what he was saying. Mark thought I was a plant or something. He really did not like me at first. Eventually, Mark and I became friends.

Natalie began working with the children's ministry at church and at the same tutoring company she had worked for before we got married. It was within a 3-minute drive from our apartment, and she worked part-time. I began attending King Solomon Lodge again. Our schedules were easy. I worked Monday through Friday and was home by 1600. Natalie worked part-time at her job, eventually becoming full-time and working at the front desk. She worked Monday through Thursday and on Saturday, but only for a couple of hours.

On Monday nights, I would be at the Lodge or at a Lodge function. We had our Stated (regular) meeting on the second

Monday of every month. Shortly after returning to the Lodge, I was appointed to the Temple Association. This is the body that governs the building funds and maintenance. I know that many people believe that Freemasons are somehow planning to run the world, but they are too disorganized for that. I was on the Temple Association before moving to California. The Temple Association was trying to decide on a color for the dining hall when I left. When I returned 2 years later, they were still trying to decide on what color to paint the dining hall. Needless to say, the Masons are not going to be running the world anytime soon.

The first weekend in May, the weekend before Mother's Day, I took Natalie out of town to Leavenworth, Washington. Leavenworth is a Bavarian village in Eastern Washington. The town has a couple of stores that sell Christmas decorations all year long and tons of cute little stores. On our drive there, we got caught in whiteout conditions due to rain. The rain was so heavy that we could not see the lines painted on the highway, but we arrived safely Thursday night. We stayed at a hotel within walking distance of the downtown area. We had the entire top floor, their bridal suite. During our visit, I picked up a musical clock for Natalie. We spent Friday and Saturday walking around town and shopping before heading home later in the afternoon.

When we returned home, my mom was in a particularly prickly mood. She thought it was Mother's Day weekend and thought we had abandoned her. My mom will do this when someone is not willing to cater to her desires. My mom got herself so worked up that she ended up in a rehab facility at one point. You see, my mom is bipolar and schizophrenic. When she is on her medications, she is fine. But after a bit, she begins to feel better and no longer thinks that she needs them. Then she spirals out of control, and she does not realize it until she is in either a manic or depressive state. She also has an issue with the iron in her blood. When her iron levels drop, she becomes dizzy and may pass out. This is why I did not want her to drive. Well, when we came home on Saturday, she was in one of her moods. She had decided that we had abandoned her on Mother's Day, which was the following weekend, and so she was going to make us suffer. I was done playing her games, but Natalie was still trying to be nice to her.

Right before we took a trip for Natalie's birthday, my mom ended up in the rehabilitation facility, claiming that she got dizzy every time she looked up and to the side. Her therapist quickly found out that this was not the case and that my mom was faking it, but she still spent two weeks in the facility before they discharged her.

Meanwhile, in February, I purchased two motorcycles. The first was a Honda Goldwing 1200 Interstate. It was an older model, but Natalie felt safe riding on the back of it because of the high seat and padding all around it. Later, I bought VTX1800 from Brother Mason, who needed to sell it quickly due to his pending divorce. I rode both of those to our apartment in the freezing rain. February in Western Washington is no joke. After buying these motorcycles, I joined the Sons of Hiram. This is a Masonic Riding Club, but more on this later.

Most of the year passed quietly for us. I was doing well at work and had gotten some projects under control. I had a few of the employees, who knew that I was a man of faith, approach me about spiritual counseling and prayer requests. I had one employee who was coming up on the third-year anniversary of his daughter's passing. He was struggling with his family telling him to "get over it" because he was beginning to forget what she looked like. His brother, who also worked for me, asked me to visit his family in the hospital. His twin babies were struggling after being born prematurely. In both cases, I did what I could to help them. All of this was happening while I was still being deluged with ads about seminaries and theological degrees.

In June, I approached pastor Chuck about all of this. He and I made an appointment for the two of us to sit down and discuss. I related to him much of what had occurred to me during my time in California and what had been happening since we returned to Washington. Chuck said, "If you can do anything else, do it!" I told him that I wish I could, but God kept putting people in my path, seeking direction, understanding, and prayer. They wanted to hear what I had learned and thought about given topics. I did not think that God was going to let this go. Chuck recommended that I investigate the Ministerial Preparation Program, MPP, offered through various Nazarene educational institutions. I began my coursework with Nazarene Bible College shortly after this.

When I was at Federal Way Naz previously, I had asked Chuck how the denomination felt about Masons. I knew that many denominations had varying feelings about Masons but was unclear about how the Nazarene felt about them. At that time, back in 2014, Chuck said that he had no idea as the question had never come up before. This time, after talking to me, Chuck went to the District Superintendent with the question. Freemasonry is one of those fraternal orders that are specifically named in the church manual as being inappropriate for Nazarene to participate in. This meant that I would never be allowed into any type of leadership position within the Church of the Nazarene. That was fine with me, as I really believed that I was called to be a non-denominational preacher. I had never considered being the spiritual leader of any church at this point.

Around this same time, I came home to have Natalie, who was content living a transitional lifestyle, tell me that she could see us putting down roots and buying a house at some point in the future. This caught me off guard because we had talked about this very issue. Natalie enjoyed living in an apartment, knowing that she could pick up and move on to something else with minimal hassles when necessary. Well, a few days later, we received a mailer about a new neighborhood just a little south of us. It was for LGI homes. We talked about it, and I booked an appointment to see the homes they had. We were not looking to buy at the time, but we were curious about pricing and amenities so we would know what to look for in a few years when we were ready. We went down to the Summerwood neighborhood on Saturday. It was about the same distance from where I worked, just on the south side of it. We toured a couple of the models, and before we knew it, we were giving them $1000 earnest money and signing paperwork. In our defense, Natalie and I never thought we would be approved because we had been turned down by several timeshares previously. But God had other plans.

Not long after this, my grandmother decided to liquidate part of the trust my grandfather had set up for the kids. Because my father had passed away 20 years earlier, his interest in trust would be divided among his surviving children: my three sisters and me. This meant that we each would receive 1/16 of the liquidated items. I was not expecting much, as I was never concerned with any type of inheritance, and we were surprised throughout this endeavor. I did not come all at once, but every time someone came in, I expected that to be the end of it. And God had other plans.

The house we had signed paperwork for would be ready by the end of November, which was perfect because our apartment lease was up in the middle of December. Every week or so, the mortgage company would call me and ask me to pay off specific bills. Natalie had her school debt; I had some credit card and auto loan debt. When they called, I would look at the debt they wanted us to pay, and often, we would have just received something from my grandmother that would take care of that debt. We were able to pay Natalie's college tuition and much of my debt quickly, based on this happening. We even managed to pay off my car loan, which was the first time I had ever owned, outright, a car I had bought brand new. This whole time, Natalie and I were waiting for the call that would end all of this, but it never came. The mortgage company sold us a house! Praise God.

Ironically, this also led to the worst argument Natalie and I ever had: me paying her tuition. She was mad at me. She felt that this was her debt and that I should not have used my inheritance to pay it off. When I got Natalie to calm down, we talked through this issue. I explained to her that we needed to pay this off to qualify for the loan. Waiting for her to pay it off over the next several months would disqualify us from the house, and she would pay even more in interest than we were already paying. She was not happy about it, but she finally accepted that I had already done this. We would also visit the homesite on the weekend, praying over the home being built, the workers on the property, and the neighborhood in general. We were not praying that we would be the owners but rather that the owners of the home would be a blessing to their community and to those they encountered. We still did not believe that we would ultimately end up in the house.

Somewhere along the way, Natalie and I began to pray that if God wanted us to live there, that He would find a way for us to spend our first Thanksgiving in Washington in this new home. Our house was scheduled to be ready for move-in on November 30th. New construction in Washington is typically delayed by a couple of weeks. Weeks went by, and we continued to pay down debt and pray over the property. Once the framework went in, Natalie and I wrote Scripture verses on the exposed struts and beams as we prayed.

On Labor Day weekend, Natalie's brother Daniel came to pick up her parents' car. They were moving back to California from Jericho and would need the car once they got here. That meant that we would only have one car, but luckily, we lived close enough for Natalie to walk to work. I would pick her up after her shift and bring her home. It was an enjoyable way to break up the monotony of schoolwork and get to spend a few minutes with my bride. Sometimes, we would go out to dinner. Other times, we just came home and ate whatever I made. As the date for our home to be ready got closer, Natalie and I decided to go try and find a car for her that we could afford. She reached out to her Facebook friends and was told about a local car dealership where one of her friends had worked several years ago. We went down on Saturday to look at what they had. They had a cute little Volvo that Natalie liked. It was great on gas, and the price was right. We had the money. Thank you, Grandma, but the bank had already closed at this point. I needed to call them to be able to either raise the limit on how much I could take from the ATM or on the purchase limit if he ran it as a credit card. I told him I would not be able to do anything until Monday. He then asked if I could write a check. Write a check? For a car purchase? What kind of dealer took a check in 2017? Because Natalie knew one of his former employees, who he was fond of because of her work ethic, this man considered us like family and was willing to take a check from us for the car. Natalie got her car that day. I dare you to tell me that this is not God at work in our lives!

On November 3rd, the Friday after we purchased the car for Natalie, I received a call from our loan agent asking that Natalie and I come to the office on the 6th to sign some paperwork. I let my boss, Tyson, know what we needed to do. Tyson had been supportive of allowing me the time to take care of things through this process, and this was no different. On the 6th,

Natalie and I took possession of our new home 24 days before it had been scheduled to be ready. From what I could tell, this was unheard of. We would get to celebrate Thanksgiving in a new home.

Over the next few weeks, Natalie and I would swing by the apartment, picking up items and taking them down to our new home. We left my mom in the apartment because the house did not yet have cable or internet services, and my mom is addicted to her tablet and phone, both of which needed internet. Right before Thanksgiving, we rented a truck, loaded up everything that was left over, and got it down to our new house. Everything was unpacked and ready for Thanksgiving, even if we did have minimal decorations on our walls. My son, Gareth, came to spend Thanksgiving with us. I drove up to get him Tuesday, I think, in the evening. While I was driving back to our house that evening, I received a call from Natalie that she was taking my mother to the emergency room. Apparently, she had fallen earlier in the week while we were at work and had not said anything to Natalie or me until now. I got home around 2000, dropped off my son, and ran to the hospital to take care of my mother. She could not understand why Natalie and I were upset with her over this. We got home after 0100, and I got up for work at 0500.

Thanksgiving was fun. Gareth, Natalie, and I went to Cabella's to get our picture with Santa. This was the first year that we did this, and it has become an annual tradition for us. I got to spend a few days with my son, and we had a lot of fun deciding how to organize furniture in our living room, seeing a movie, and just spending time together. Our photo with

Santa is one of my favorites. Gareth is a huge fan of DC Comics. He had a Superman shirt underneath his button-up shirt. In both the picture I took at our table and the one we got at Cabela's, he is "ripping" open his shirt to reveal the giant "S" on his t-shirt. It got a big smile from the photographer at Cabela's.

It was in December that Natalie and I purchased a couch set for our house and had it delivered. It was also in December that I went through the degrees for York Rite, Royal Arch Masons, the Council of Cryptic Masons, and the Commandery of Knight Templar during the Grand Master's weekend conferral. Each of these bodies is comprised of several degrees, each of which must be progressed through individually before going on to the next one. Knight Templar is the highest degree in the Your Rite and is limited to Christian Masons, as you must swear to defend the faith against all enemies of the faith. Some of the rituals were weird, but based on the source material, it makes sense. On December 9th, I was installed as the Chaplain at King Solomon Lodge.

We had a white Christmas, of sorts, that year. My mom, who hates Christmas (how is this possible?), was as miserable as ever while Natalie tried to play peacemaker with her. I was simply over this foolishness from my mother, who seemed to never stop complaining about something. We were still attending Federal Way Nazarene, and my mom went with us. Natalie and I had spent much of the time in our new home discussing God's calling on our lives and had formed A Place for All, our ministry to others. I even commissioned a logo for it. The logo turned out great. It is a tree, sprouting up out of a

Bible, with Matthew 13:31-32 spelled out in its roots. In the tree, there are birds and several people standing beneath the tree. It represents faith in God's Word, which comes to us from Scripture and provides a covering for true believers. The Scripture reference is the Mustard Seed parable. That little seed, hearing the Word, sprouts into belief and a changed life, which then gives us guidance to live out God's will in our lives.

God has blessed us since Natalie and I met, started dating, got engaged, married, and then moved to a new State, all in the first year. In this second year, the blessing continued with us buying a new home and making it our own, as well as with a car purchase that would have been unheard of at the time outside of a small town where everyone knew everyone else. We were blessed in that both of us had good jobs, good friends, and a good church. It was also around this time that Natalie and I decided to step away from the Nazarene Church. With my ongoing involvement with Masonry, I could not in good conscience stay with the Nazarene, and I did not want to put pastor Chuck in an awkward position because of me. Thus began our church shopping again. God was still doing miraculous work in our lives, and we give Him the glory for all of it to this day.

2018 – New Horizons and the Loss of Family

In January, we decided to get a puppy. I had grown up with dogs and missed owning one. In my previous marriages, we had lived in either apartments or a mobile home, apart from the home Deborah and I rented in Tacoma. Because of this, I was never able to have a dog for long, if at all. Deborah and I had a dog for about 2 weeks in Tacoma until he was stolen from our yard while she was taking a nap. Maddy had a dog in my mobile home, but it was a small, yappy little thing, not a real dog. So, here was my first real chance as an adult to have a dog again. We picked up Micah on January 17th. It was a sketchy transaction from the beginning. We met the owners (breeders) in the parking lot of the Bingo Hall in Auburn. They had several excuses as to why they could not keep him, but they honestly looked like tweakers. I am not saying that they were, but they gave off that vibe. I paid $200 for Micah, and they asked me to meet the following week to get his shot records and the final shots he needed. We scheduled an appointment with a vet to get him real shots and a shot record. They could not remember when Micah was born, so Natalie and I decided he had been born on our wedding anniversary. Micah is a rottweiler pug mix. He is the size of a large pug but has the coloring and face of a rottweiler. The only other pug in him is his goofy smile and pug tail. He is adorable.

In January, I was also approached by the wife of a friend to begin attending the local Bethel of Job's Daughters. This is a

Masonic organization for young ladies. Girls need to be at least 12 years old and sponsored by a Master Mason. There used to be a requirement that they be related to them by blood or marriage, but now, they just need to be sponsored by one. As a Masonic organization, they were required to have a Master Mason on the advisory board who held the position of Bethel Guardian. My friend was the Bethel Guardian for several groups in our area, and his wife wanted him to take a step back from being involved in so many groups. I did not know it at the time, but she wanted me to take over as the Bethel Guardian for this group.

During the late Winter and early Spring, I would travel to several different Lodges to support them. I was there for their Installation of Officers, various Degrees being given to initiates and members as they rose through the ranks, and then our various fundraisers throughout the year. I got to know several of the members of these Lodges, and many of them belonged to the Sons of Hiram Riding Club. Many of the members of the club became close friends of mine and remained as such even after I left Masonry.

In February, during one of my many trips to Enumclaw, I noticed that the Summit Church had Saturday evening services. We decided to go for a visit. We enjoyed it there, and with them having service on Saturday evening, it allowed us time to visit other churches on Sunday to get to know them better. The Summit had a wonderful pastor, Ross, who was joined by an amazing ministry staff. The downside was that everything was separated along gender lines for adults. They had a men's ministry, Joshua's Men, and a women's ministry, Women of the Word, but nothing for couples to do together. It was at this church that I met Brett (Raz), Dan, Patrick, Dave, and many others.

Part of A Place for All is reaching out to those around us, helping them to better understand the Gospel message, and getting them into a Bible-preaching church where they can grow in their relationship with Christ. As such, Natalie and I spent much of our time meeting people, bringing relief to the homeless, and just listening to others' struggles. I usually did this with a clerical collar on. Between that collar and my Sons of Hiram vest, I would engage in many conversations around both groups, Masons and Christians. All these conversations would end up talking about Jesus and asking if the other party(s) had a sanctifying relationship with Christ. I would use anything I had to open those conversations. Natalie and I would, on occasion, drive around and hand out food, water, toothpaste, socks, and even blankets to the homeless. It was at this point that I began to hand out small copies of the Bible as well.

In February, the Sons have their annual meeting. It is at this meeting that we vote on officers, decide what rides we want to go on throughout the upcoming year, and decide on the charitable groups we want to support. I was voted in as the Secretary of the group at this meeting. I was not really offered a choice. They said I could decline, but that would mean that the current secretary, who had moved to Oregon, would still be in the position despite not being around. I grudgingly accepted.

Natalie's parents came out for a visit at Easter. Gene loves Easter baskets, so Natalie made sure to get them both baskets. I have never celebrated Easter since my kids grew up, but watching the pure joy on Gene's face was worth it all. While here, Natalie and her parents made several trips around Washington, visiting various friends of her parents. They only came out for a short visit this time. This was Gene's first visit and Cecelia's second time with us in Washington.

Around Memorial Day, Maple Valley has a big parade and festival in the park. Natalie, Micha, and I went to watch the parade before walking around the festival. The parade was fun for Natalie and me. The sons of the owner at Bellmont Cabinets were there with minibikes and kids, riding in the parade. We got to see a lot of great groups in the parade. Sadly, for Micah, this included a high school band with loud drums. Micah has never been comfortable around loud noises ever since. All of us enjoyed the festival, though. Natalie and I looked at all the artisan booths, and Micah got to sniff everything and got treats and pets from many who were there.

One Saturday morning, I headed out to King Solomon Lodge in Auburn. I took care of what I needed to at the Lodge and made a quick pitstop at the Safeway there. While there, I had to use the restroom. As I was doing what I needed to do, a gentleman walked out of the stall, saw my cut, which I was wearing, and started talking to me about motorcycles. When I turned around, he saw my collar. It was at this point that he broke down and started crying, asking me for help. I was initially wary of his intentions, but I could not deny that his anxiety was real. We stepped out of the restroom and continued our talk in a more dignified area. He laid his life out for me to see. He had been in and out of rehab and jail; he was living with his mother and had gotten drunk last night in a spat of anger and depression. His mother locked him out of the house. I drove him to his mother's house, but no one was home. I ended up taking him to Harbor View Hospital to see if they could find him a treatment facility. While I was there, several of the other patients asked to speak to me, so I spent a fair amount of time running around to different hospital beds. Meanwhile, my mom got dizzy and fell. Natalie took her to Good Sam's in Puyallup. Apparently, I was destined to be in a hospital that morning and afternoon. I left the gentleman at the hospital after they told me that they found a detox facility for him. I had left a message for his mother, who called me back the following day. I spent the next several days visiting with his mother and sister while he was in jail for one of his many parole violations.

Natalie's parents came back out for another visit this summer. Turns out that they had other friends who lived in or were visiting Washington, which is why they came. They expected Natalie to drive them all over the place to visit these friends of theirs, some of whom Natalie knew as well. Natalie drove to Silverdale at least 8 times in a 2-week period. Not a big deal, except she needed to go across a toll bridge each time when she came home. It was also at this time that things began to go south with my mother. She had become entitled, wanting us to be there when she needed us and for us to be out of her life when she thought she was doing well. Natalie and I ended up in two different emergency rooms in different counties one day. I was with a man I had just met who was struggling with his alcohol addiction. He had fallen off the wagon the night before while she was in the hospital by our house with my mother because her iron levels were too low.

In June of 2018, my cousin Jared went home to Jesus. He had been diagnosed with stage 4 cancer in 2017 and finally succumbed to death's embrace. July 28th was the memorial ceremony for him. I drove out to Meridian a couple of days before to be with family. I saw my aunt and uncle, his sister Christy, and several other family members I had not seen in a while. Many of them had no idea that I had accepted Jesus and were overjoyed to hear about it. While I was there, my Uncle Dan told me about Chaplain Fellowship Ministries International. It was a group that he had joined and been licensed through. I decided to check them out once I returned to Washington, which I did on Sunday. It was the first time I had missed being in an actual church since 2014 on a Sunday.

I returned to work the following day. I still loved working at Bellmont, but it had gotten tougher to be there. My boss, who really did not like me for some reason, seemed to find fault with me on almost a daily basis. I had my employees, who I loved, but there were some who felt that they saw greener pastures elsewhere. This meant that I was spending a lot of time on the floor, training and helping to guide several new hires while also dealing with equipment malfunctions and trying to get machinery that had long been out of service back up and running. The stress was starting to get to me.

In September, I was also installed as the Associate Bethel Guardian for our Jobies Bethel. It was a small group that was trying to grow. They had stalled out on bringing in younger girls a couple of years ago, and then the majority aged out, which left us with about five or six girls left in the group. In Jobies, the girls serve 6-month terms. At the end of each term, they hold elections. The adults are supposed to guide the girls to make sure that they are ready to step into the next role. The Bethel Guardian was the mother of the Honored Queen, who had served multiple terms, as the other girls were deemed not fit to step up into their next role despite filling their current role for over a year. My role was to ensure that all the girls had the opportunity to learn and grow so that they could all step up the next term. My time with Jobies lasted about a year, and I had to walk away from them when I walked away from Masonry.

In October, the Sons of Hiram performed security at a haunted forest as a fundraiser. The forest is held at the Royal Arch Park and is staffed by various Masonic organizations. We did security and medical response. All the scare sets were staffed by kids from Rainbow Girls, Job's Daughters, and DeMolay. In addition to this, we had several adults who came out to staff ticketing and vending, as well as acted as runners and escorts for the kids who needed bathroom breaks and parking control. We also had outside vendors who came in to sell items they made, do face paintings, and whatever else the committee thought would help to improve the enjoyment for the patrons. Each group was paid from the proceeds based on the number of hours worked by each group. I did not know it yet, but this was to be my last year at the park. They had brought in locals to do tarot card readings, which was just not something I could abide by. Up until this year, the owner of the park had a standing rule that they would not allow any depiction of demons or devils at the event and would not have anything pointing toward witchcraft because of his deep religious beliefs. Somehow, the committee got around this. By the midpoint of the season, I was done with this nonsense.

After my return from Idaho, I began to read about CFMI and reached out to the director. He and I exchanged several emails and phone calls. Finally, after several interviews, I was granted membership in their organization, which includes licensing and ordination as a Chaplain. Usually, there is a period where they observe and test you, asking you to complete several courses in their program, yet after the interviews, they had deemed that my experience was beyond most of those seeking membership. Not sure that I agree with them, but I do thank them and God for their confidence. I was ordained with them in November of 2018. It was at this time that Natalie and I first attempted to begin a small Bible study in our home. Attendance was haphazard, often just being Natalie and myself, but we were faithful to have food ready for anyone who might show up and then to study Scripture after dinner. It is something that we both enjoy.

In November of 2018, I joined Crescent Lodge in Enumclaw, Washington. The presiding Master of the Lodge was a friend of mine from the Sons and someone I had grown to respect. In December 2018, I was also installed as the Senior Deacon at King Solomon. This would be my final office in the Masonic world.

2018 ended with me serving my mother with eviction papers. I had asked her to move out during the summer as her attitude was starting to negatively impact my marriage. One night, when I was extremely angry with her, I sat up for hours writing and rewriting a letter to explain things to her. I did this because my mom never came out of her room and avoided talking to us at all times. When we moved to Washington, my mom needed new hearing aids. I bought those for her, and she had promised to pay us back $50 a month until the $3000 was paid in total. She paid for about 6 months, but I let it go, knowing that money was tight for her. She was also supposed to pay us $100 or so in rent every month, but I am forgetting the exact amount. We only did that because she needed to show that she was paying rent for her benefits. Both were at my mother's insistence. She had stopped paying rent in June. In addition to all of this, my mom was stealing from us. She would see things around the house and would claim that they were hers. She would then take them up to her room. She even stole a Corningware pan from a friend of ours who brought us dinner one night. My mom had not had one of these in years.

I laid all of this out in that letter, in addition to telling my mom that I was still upset with her for denying that I existed when I was 17 and she was drunk. She had gone out to a New Year's Eve party with a neighbor, gotten falling down drunk, and he had called me at home to come pick up my mother. When I got there, as we were trying to put her in my car, she kept asking who I was and where my sister was. The neighbor told her that he had called her son, to which she said, "Matt is too young to drive. Call Suzanne!" When we explained that he had called her son Shane, she repeatedly said that she did not have a son named Shane and that Suzanne was the only one old enough to drive. I had buried that event deep down and told her the next morning that I forgave her, but I had never worked through my emotions about that event. That she was drunk should not have made her forget about the only one of her three children who was always there to help her, but it did. By 2018, I was done hiding my emotions over this event and needed to talk to her about it. Her response? "You are not over that yet? It happened 20 years ago. Deal with it and move on, but I am done talking about it." Well, I guess I am, too. I served her with eviction papers to move out of my house, or I would take her to court to have her removed.

My mom asked me to give her until January, which I agreed to. It was painful, but she finally realized I was serious when we received a notice from our HOA about a car parked in front of our house for several days. This was my mom's car, which she had gone out and purchased against my wishes. My mom's medical condition meant that she should not drive as she could pass out behind the wheel anytime. As such, I told her that she could not park in the driveway or the garage. So, she parked it right in front of the house, violating HOA rules. When I received the letter with a fine notice, I wrote an email to the HOA management company. I informed her that I had a car, and my wife had a car, but unless my dogs were driving this vehicle, no one living at my house was driving the vehicle in question. This prompted her to call me, tell me how funny she found my email, and let me know that she had removed the fine from our record. My mom moved out on January 1, 2019, leaving our house unlocked, the security system disarmed, and her room a mess, all because she was mad at me.

2019 – Living by the Grace of God

As I have already mentioned, our year started off with a bang when my mother moved away. We never heard from her again. In fact, over the years, I have attempted to reach out to her about unimportant things, and she has responded by telling me to "F off" and hanging up. She has blocked me on her phone and on social media, which is fine with me. How she left her room was not.

When my mom moved out, she left several items behind, including things that she insisted be brought to Washington from California, which did make me a little mad. I spent the next few weeks moving her stuff from her room out to our garage. She was kind enough to leave her mattress, which had been Natalie's bed when she and I met. The mattress was now useless because it had fresh fecal matter and urine on it. I went to clean the bathroom that my mother used, and there was dried fecal matter all over it. The walls in my mother's room – fecal matter and body oil stains. It was disgusting. I had to leave the window open to air it out and used our carpet cleaner several times to remove the other unknown stains that were on the carpet. Because I had my mother on a lease, I decided to hold on to her stuff for 90 days before getting rid of it. It was all trash. Her room later became my office.

In February, things had finally reached a boiling point for me at work. I was tired of being stressed and anxious when I went into a job I once loved. Right around my birthday, Natalie and I went out to dinner. I told her about what was going on and why I was feeling so stressed. At one point, I looked at her and told her I was done. I was going to go in and give my notice. Immediately, a weight was lifted from my shoulders, and I was at peace about work and life. True to form, I went to work on that next Monday, asked for some time with Tyson, and handed him my resignation letter. I told him what my last day would be and that if he desired me to leave before that, that would be fine as well. Tyson accepted my resignation and immediately sought to replace me with one of his other supervisors.

On my last day there, Tyson and Jarred called me into their office. We sat down and talked about my leaving. They kept asking me where I was going next. I did not have anything lined up, so I told them so. I was planning to spend some time at home to reflect on what led me to this place before seeking new employment. Right before Tyson dismissed me from his office, he told me that he knew I was never given a fair chance. I was given a team with broken equipment and a few tenured employees. He knew that a lot had been asked of me and that I had done a lot more than he had been willing to admit. I also knew because he told me on several occasions that he did not like me and never wanted me for the position. I walked away happy. I honestly thought I would find another position easily, but I was wrong.

Days turned into weeks, which turned into months. After being depressed for a couple of weeks, I began to reach out and apply to various positions. Sadly, many of them wanted me to work a rotating schedule, including Sundays. I went to a few interviews, and when they asked about me working on

Sundays, I would tell them that was not a viable option for me. As a Christian, I needed to gather with the Church in corporate worship on that day. That quickly thinned the opportunities for me.

In May of this year, I went to work for a glass manufacturer in Renton. It was an overnight shift, scheduled to be 2100-0600. Sadly, from day 1, the shift ran from 1900-0600, 6 days a week. I worked Sunday night to Saturday morning. It was grueling. I barely saw Natalie, drove 60 miles a day, and was always exhausted. The way they operated made no sense and was counterintuitive to how things should be done. The graveyard shift was set as a catch-up shift, and they were always behind in orders. Every day, dozens of orders would go past due because of them trying to catch up with previous past-due orders. It only lasted a month, at which point I had an anxiety attack and knew I could no longer do this job. I promptly left the company.

It was shortly after this that I noticed a position was still open in which I was interested. I had not applied for it because it was asking for skills and experience I did not have, but I thought I would go ahead and apply anyway. It was for the Quality Environmental Health and Safety (QEHS) Manager at a global company within the paper industry. I had the EHS experience but not the in-depth Quality experience they wanted. I Had noticed this job back when my job search began but had ignored it due to my limited fulfillment of their requirements. After a series of interviews for this position, I started working there on July 31st.

My first day on the job was interesting. The General Manager was off that day, but they wanted me to start before the end of the month so that my benefits would kick in sooner. When the GM returned, she informed me that we were overdue for a "surprise" inspection by the state Environmental Agency. They eventually showed up in November. At the beginning of September, I went to Portland for ISO training. Certification as an ISO Auditor was a condition of employment.

My role was simple on paper. I was responsible for conducting audits for quality, safety, and environmental compliance, in addition to compiling and submitting all regulatory reports required to show our compliance. If we had a paper roller come in with a defect, or if a defect was created during our servicing of the roll, I was to conduct a Root Cause Corrective Action (RCCA) of the roll in question and try to develop a path forward to prevent this from happening again. Sounds simple enough, right? Well, the GM saw my position differently. She wanted me to ensure that nothing was our fault and that any issues found would always point back to misuse or neglect on the part of our customers. She wanted me to generate a pretty report that looked good and to baffle everyone by talking in circles and avoiding accepting blame. She felt that my position was unnecessary other than to fulfill regulatory requirements.

I liked this job because of the people and that it was only about a ½ hour drive each way. I was in around 6-630 and left by 1600. I never had to work on the weekends and was only asked to work late one week when I had contractors on site conducting some cleanup. I got along well with everyone, but the same could not be said about others. The GM operated through fear and intimidation, but everyone was used to it.

In September, my daughter got married. In June, she had asked me to perform at her wedding because she was having trouble finding someone who would do it. My daughter does not have a relationship with Christ and does not attend any church. Her husband was a nice gentleman who treated her well. Sadly, their marriage broke up a year later.

By the time I went to work for this company, I had effectively been out of work for 5 months since I left the cabinet shop. We fell 1 ½ months behind on our mortgage payments during this time. I was sending in what I could, when I could, and had even worked out a repayment plan with the lender. Under that repayment plan, and per their advice, I was sending in partial payments every payday. Those partial payments were supposed to be applied immediately, but I later found out that none of them were applied until they had enough for full payment. This meant that it continued to be past due, as they applied it to the oldest past due first. By December, they had threatened to begin eviction proceedings against us.

Over the summer, I began to question my involvement with Masonry. I felt as if God was pulling me out of it. I no longer found the same sense of comradery outside of the Sons and began to question many of the ideas espoused within the Lodge. In August, I submitted my demit to both lodges. Several members of King Solomon reached out to me directly to talk about my reasons for leaving. They reminded me that I could remain a member at no cost since I was a Life Member. After some thought, I asked the Secretary of the Lodge not to read it at the next meeting, but he did. It bothered me that he could not follow simple requests, but it did not bother me that I was out. I then contacted the Secretary at Crescent, asking that he remove my demit and transfer my life membership to that Lodge. It took 3 months, but they were able to get that done. Keeping my membership saved Natalie and me.

In December, with nowhere else to turn, I reached out to my Lodge and Washington Masonic Charities. I had a good relationship with the director of the charity from our past dealings. Between the Lodge, the Charity, and a friend of mine, who was the Worshipful Master of the Lodge, Natalie and I were able to get everything caught up on our mortgage in January 2020. Sadly, Covid also became a global pandemic in 2019. What started as possibly the flu became much bigger in early 2020.

2020 – The Pandemic Changes the Landscape

January started off with a massive storm. This storm brought several inches of snow to the Puget Sound region of Washington. One morning, while heading to work, I decided to take the safest route I could. With the amount of ice on the roads, I wanted to avoid as many hills as possible. The route I took would take me down one hill, but the rest of the way would be relatively flat, with only a mild incline as I arrived at work. The downside to this is that the main stretch of road I would be on had no streetlights. It was icy out. I even slid through one stoplight despite driving less than 20 miles per hour. When I hit that main stretch, it was dark and treacherous. Up ahead, I noticed faint yellow flashing lights, but they were spread out enough that I knew they did not belong to the same vehicle. As I got closer, I noticed slight outlines in the distance, indicating at least two different vehicles, both at odd angles. I reduced my speed even further, and as the car in front of me took shape, I began to slowly apply my brakes to slow down even more. The ice was thick here, and I soon began to slide on it. Remaining calm, I turned my wheel, which caused my car to turn sideways. I eventually came to a full stop about three feet away from this other vehicle. We were side by side at this point. It looked like the driver of this car, and another one, had some type of an accident that turned them both sideways, with the third vehicle coming to a rest about 20 feet away, facing head-on to the car I was next to. I quickly checked in with both drivers, who assured me that they were ok, and then I finished driving on to my work with no further incident. That was fun.

Work at my company was progressing well. Natalie was working in Christian Education, and we were excited to participate in both churches we attended. Other than our year starting off stressful with the possibility of eviction, everything was going well. In March, the governor of Washington began to implement some strict guidelines around the looming Covid-19 pandemic. Everyone had to learn how to socially distance themselves in public. All non-essential businesses were closed, and those of us who were deemed essential had to go to work while the majority were paid by the government to stay home. Grocery stores put stickers on the ground to remind people to always stay at least 6 feet apart. Some even put up plexiglass dividers between customers and the cashiers. It seemed like no one questioned the stupidity of it all, at least where we lived. My company asked me to put certain practices in place that were simply impractical and unnecessary. Most of the employees refused to comply, so we did not unless someone came for a visit.

The Grand Lodge of Washington closed all Lodges until further notice. This meant no in-person meetings and that no business could be conducted. The Grand Lodge did allow the officers of the Lodge to meet via Zoom and authorize payments for regular, recurring items so that the utilities and other things continue to be paid. By this time, I was no longer involved with much of what was going on in the Lodge. Other than the Sons, I had little to do with Masonry as I had resigned from Jobies, resigned from King Solomon, and was a member in name only at Crescent. I had also resigned and submitted my demit to all other Masonic organizations other than the Sons and Crescent. The only role I had was as the Secretary of the Sons, from which I resigned in May. I went to one last gathering, asked to talk to the officers of the club, told them of my resignation, and handed in my cut. I did this because, in March, I joined the Men of Acts Motorcycle Missionary group. It was a group I had found on social media, and I liked what they stood for. I reached out to Wolfman and talked with him. By the end of March, I had received my patches. After a few months of prayer, I found that I could no longer affiliate myself with Masonic teachings. While not a religious group, they did have religious leanings, many of which I disagreed with.

Covid brought out the worst in people. Because of masking mandates, many felt that this gave them free rein to commit crimes since their identities were hidden behind masks. In Washington, we saw a drastic uptick in robbery and assault, and with the lockdowns that the governor ordered, we also saw a 300% uptick in spousal crimes. At the end of May, George Floyd was detained by law enforcement officers in Minneapolis. During his detainment, Mr. George died. Many people in the US felt that he was killed by the officers who detained him, with physical restraint holds that they used, including one officer who detained him with a knee to his throat. The media fueled the fires of protest by publishing the most outlandish stories about the event. The outrage many felt eventually sparked protests around the country.

In Seattle, on June 1st, protesters went into a neighborhood in Seattle and established what became known as the Capital Hill Occupied Protest (CHOP) zone. Protesters took over the East Precinct of the Seattle Police Department after the PD abandoned the building. Protesters had originally been met by police in riot gear, but the leadership of Seattle ordered that police retreat and surrender the area to the protesters. The protesters included elements of the Black Lives Matter (BLM) movement and several gangs local to the area. Inside the zone, with no police presence, several people were assaulted, businesses burglarized, and it eventually led to the death of at least 2 people. When the police finally retook the area, it resulted in the arrest and detainment of at least 40 people.

During the summer of 2020, protests were happening all over Western Washington. Seed of Life, being an African American church, participated in many of the protests. While the church insisted on wearing masks, even when they held outdoor services, they felt free to gather with these protests without wearing masks. I am not sure what changed between the two events, but it was clear that they were not thinking this through. In July, while at the church for corporate worship, it became clear to me that I might be more of a hindrance to the other members because of the color of my skin. After the service, as they were getting ready to go and join a local protest, some of the members were giving me dirty looks. I felt uncomfortable. Natalie and I went home and discussed it. She noticed the same thing, and by the end of the week, I met with pastor Paul and told him that Natalie and I would be stepping away for a while. He understood. Church shopping again?

Eventually, Natalie and I settled back at Federal Way Nazarene. It was late September by this point, but we had visited several other churches in our area by then. None of them felt right. Once back at Fed, pastor Chuck pulled Natalie aside to ask her if I was going to have a problem with a certain member. Chuck had heard some rumors about why we left a few years earlier and was concerned that there might be some unresolved issues between this person and me. Natalie told him to ask me, so he did. The rumors Chuck had heard were false. We had not left the church because of the member in question. In fact, I had told Chuck why we felt we needed to step away. Chuck was good with my explanation.

I began working with the Men's group, who I had continued to meet with monthly during our absence, and Natalie went back to working with the Children's ministry. The former Children's pastor, who liked Natalie so much, had left that church and was working at her own church plant. The new director was happy to have Natalie, but all the children were gone. In October, Natalie and I placed membership with the church again.

I have mentioned that the GM at my work operates through intimidation and threats. Well, in September, she called me on my cellphone while I was on lunch and driving. It is a violation of company policy to talk on the phone, even with hands-free devices, while driving. The GM proceeded to use excessive vulgar language toward me. It was bad enough that, after I returned to the work site, I wrote out a long email, citing the violation and how I felt being attacked by her in such a manner. I had planned to send that to Human Resources but sent it to her instead. The next morning, when she finally got to work, she asked me to have a conversation with her. During our talk, she apologized profusely for her language and behavior. She attempted to blame it on the work environment and her feeling as if she always needed to prove herself to others. After this, she toned down her language around me, but I did start documenting things I saw and heard involving her. I had a feeling that this would become important soon.

Le, my Project Manager at work, became a close friend. Nothing inappropriate, but it was someone I could use as a sounding board for work issues, and she did the same with me. After one particularly bad encounter that she had with the GM, I told her that I was documenting things like that, which I had witnessed or heard firsthand. I recommended that she do the same in case something happened. We never shared notes, but I knew that she began doing the same. Over the course of time, the GM became even worse. She would show up late, yell at the employees, and try to make everyone miserable. One of our lathe operators was forced to work most weekends to complete work over the weekend. He was the junior operator, but since the senior operator was not interested in the overtime, the junior was told that he would work to complete the work. When he requested a day off to celebrate his child's birthday, it was denied by the GM, who then took a day off to celebrate her son's birthday a few weeks later. Eventually, this would add up and cause resentment in most of the employees. The work was not all bad, though. The employees there were an excellent group. Le had taken to introducing me to visitors as the QEHS Manager and pastor. I always thought it was an interesting choice, but I let her because it brought her some sense of happiness.

Throughout 2020, Natalie and I had taken a few trips around Washington. For our anniversary, we went to visit the Stonehenge memorial in Goldendale, Washington. We took the puppies with us, who enjoyed the ride and traveled well. We spent most of the day driving because of Covid and spent the night in Winthrop. It was a long day, and it was good for us to get away for the weekend with the kids. We came back through Leavenworth and Monroe. There is a little chapel called the Wayside Chapel between Monroe and Everett. I always enjoy stopping there and just reflecting on the fact that someone placed this beautiful, 4-person chapel on the side of the road for whoever would need it. This is God at work in our world.

In November, Chuck, Scott, and I got together to discuss a new study for our Men's Ministry. Someone decided that I should lead it. We were going to do a book study on the Disciplines of a Godly Man by R. Kent Hughes. The only problem I had with this is that we only meet once a month, and the book is 19 chapters long. This would mean that we would be in this book for almost two years. The church typically suspends ministry groups for the summer and around the holidays, so this would mean that June – August and December would have no events. With a kickoff in January 2021, this would take us out to January 2023 to complete this book. While I would rather meet more frequently and try to develop ways to put the principles in the book into action, I did not want to shake things up too much. November and

December were spent getting materials in place, ordering books for our group, and developing discussion plans for us. If only I had known then what I know now. Better tools exist today than we were aware of then.

2021 – A Return to the Church of the Nazarene

In January, I returned to Nazarene Bible College as a student. I had to retake the online orientation in December, but January marked my first regular class as a returning student. It was Exploring Nazarene History and Polity. I learned a lot in this class, including much that surprised me. This class took us back to a time before the Nazarene Church was a denomination. They like to claim that, while other denominations came out of church splits, the Nazarenes come from several denominations banding together for the Nazarene Church. It was in this class that I learned about people like Phoebe Palmer and Phineas Bresee, two of the early leaders in the movement that would eventually spawn the Church of the Nazarene.

In reviewing some of my emails from 2021, I see that things were heating up at work with the GM. The GM came to me to ask about some signoffs on rolls that were still pending. I told her that I had all of them caught up except for one roll, which was still being disassembled. Apparently, she thought I was talking about a different role, one that was being covered now. I had already told her three times that the one she was asking about was good to go, but it never clicked in her mind. She had also found a Purchase Order from 2020 and wanted me to capitalize it in our system. I told her there was no problem and got to work on it. The PO had been partially received in 2020, which prompted her to call in our finance person, Wade, to continue the discussion. After our discussion, Wade asked her if she still wanted to capitalize it, to which she tried to correct him by saying that I wanted to capitalize it and that we had just wasted our time even discussing this. Her response to both was to get belligerent and scream at me over her misunderstanding of the situation.

The following week, Le approached me to tell me of an incident the day before. Le had been asked to include specific verbiage in a report. She included it and sent it to our customer sales representative, who caught an error in it. He corrected it quickly and without incident, yet the GM decided that it was appropriate to go in and scream at Le for making a mistake. Now, Le and I share a window between our offices, so anything said in one can be heard in the other. I caught bits and pieces of the original argument over this but did not know everything that had precipitated it happening. Le and I felt that the GM was being more cordial to Le this morning because she knew that she had crossed the line the day before. This would all come to a head in March.

Most of the first part of 2021 was mundane. Natalie was working at Cascade Christian Schools; we attended Federal Way Church of the Nazarene on Sunday and the Summit on Saturday evenings. I was still working for the same company. Each month, I would spend the second Saturday with the men at Federal Way and the third Saturday with the men at the Summit. It was a good schedule for us. School was going well, which led to me having questions about the Nazarene Church. Pastor Chuck and I would meet often, usually on a Saturday, to discuss my questions and for him to speak into my life through what he saw.

In 2020, I applied to be a State Ambassador for Promise Keepers. It took a long time to get settled, but I was trying to be engaged with the churches around us in this capacity. Sadly, their relaunch had been negatively impacted by the Covid pandemic, which caused them to rethink how they were going to do their kick-off and relaunch. Their focus had also shifted in that they were more focused on working with local churches to promote their events, encouraging churches to host the simulcast events, and then working with the Ambassadors to help facilitate training and encouragement to their Men's ministry at the local level. Many churches were not interested in this as too much had taken place to make these resources easily accessible to them on a regular basis. Promise Keepers could be a storehouse of information, but that same information was already available to churches at little or no cost.

The Ambassadors, under the leadership of George S, would have regular Zoom calls with each other. George and the team got along well, and we enjoyed coming together for prayer and fellowship. It was often difficult for me to be involved with the calls, but they were also calls that I looked forward to each week. I really liked the guys I was getting to know in our region. Promise Keepers tried to keep things up and running throughout 2021, but I eventually bowed out of the organization due to no interest by local churches in them.

In 2020, I had also found out about a ministry called Village Missions. This is a group that seeks to work with rural churches by supplying a full-time pastor to lead their church. The church would need to provide a place for the pastor and his family to live. The design of this is that the pastor would spend about half of their time seeing to the needs of the congregation, preparing sermons, and providing pastoral leadership to the congregation. The rest of their time would be spent in the community, getting to know people and working to spread the gospel in that community. Much of their funding would initially come from the organization Village Missions until the church was finally able to support its pastor. It is a wonderful organization, and it is one that I had hoped to join. Because of my being divorced, though, they decided to pass on me when I originally applied.

In March, the Assistant Director of the organization reached out to me. The organization had recently revised its rules, making divorce no longer an automatic disqualifying event. Because of this, he wanted me to reapply to them and go through the process. I did. It took several months, emails, and even phone calls, but I finally received the expected dismissal in June. Because of the number of divorces, I have 3, and the brief time that my wife and I had been married at this point, 5 years, they decided that they could not move forward with me, especially in a rural setting. I was okay with this as I was also working on my district licensing process with the Nazarenes.

Chuck approached me about being locally licensed with Federal Way and applying for my District License with the Washington Pacific region of the church. To begin this process, I needed to submit a Call to Ministry Form through their website. I found this and submitted it in April. I also registered and began to capture my lifelong learning hours on the Nazarene website. In June, I received an email from the District Secretary letting me know that she had received my forms and apologized for not responding sooner. I had applied while she was on vacation, and they had gotten misplaced in her inbox. Sadly, if I were going to apply for my District License, I would need to do this very quickly since they had to be in by the end of August, I think.

Part of the vetting process for a District License is the *Removal of Divorce as a Barrier to Ordination*, which is a form and an interview that must be completed before your License interview. My interview for this process was set for September 18th, 1100 - 1115 via Zoom. Now, Chuck had often joked with me that he thought it was easier for a convicted murderer to be ordained in the Nazarene Church than a divorcee. When I saw that the interview" was scheduled for a whopping 15 minutes, I felt like they had already made up their mind about me. I went into the interview on the defensive and with a less-than-ideal attitude. The Zoom format was ridiculous, but I was in a predominately liberal state who felt that Covid was worse than many of the rest of us. During the interview, I was asked many questions about events that led up to each divorce, but they seemed to ignore that all of these were before Christ. One of the women on the panel even asked me, when discussing my second divorce, if my wife had left me for a man or a woman. I could not even begin to understand what bearing that would have on the situation. I told her that she left me for another man and soon moved out of state with him and her kids. I came out of the interview not feeling like it had gone well. I received their response after what felt like weeks but were only 10 days.

Their letter included the following:

Thank you so much for taking the time out of your busy schedule to come to meet with us on Zoom about your divorce. We know that this was not an easy thing to do, and we appreciate the difficulty of discussing a delicate and painful time in your life with a group of strangers. You handled this with grace and honesty.

It was followed by an explanation that they had discussed this at length and had to come to this hard decision, yet this does not preclude me from serving in the church. They finished with a few recommendations for me:

- Intentional mentoring from someone who has been in a long-term marriage

- A lengthy commitment to a local Church of the Nazarene

- Professional counseling to help you understand patterns of behavior that affect your relationships and ministry.

I understood and agreed with the first two items, yet that third one threw me for a loop. When they say professional counseling, what do they mean, and how long do they think it should be? I reached out to the District Superintendent to ask because I was very upfront with the panel that I took responsibility for my actions and placed the blame at my own feet. I had allowed my inaction and lack of communication to influence what happened in each marriage. I did not hold anything against any of them. It just felt surreal. Of course, my initial reaction to this, while expected, was severe disappointment in being denied.

I reached out to Chuck immediately. Chuck was appalled by the results of this. It was not unexpected for him since he was on the ministerial credential board and sat in on the discussion. He did tell me that he was the lone voice who advocated for me, which was disappointing since at least one other member knew me personally. Chuck said that he would not be surprised if I were to walk away from the Nazarene Church and never look back. I told him that I was upset but that I felt God had not yet released me from serving the Nazarene Church. I was going to take a few weeks off to lick my wounds, and then I would be back. Natalie and I were absent from Federal Way for the month of October, but we returned in November with a renewed sense of vigor. Natalie participated in the Halloween City Wide event, helping to host the church booth and hand out candy. When I went to pick her up, I ran into Chuck and Rhonda, who were both impressed with how Natalie sought out the kids and engaged them. Natalie is a remarkable sight when she is in her element with kids.

2022 – A Harsh Reality Check

Pastor Chuck had already communicated to the Board that he was planning to step down at the end of April. In January, he approached Natalie and me about taking over some things within the church. He wanted Natalie to be the Children's Director under me as the Family pastor. We had no idea how this would work, but we agreed. Chuck asked us to submit a resume for the Board to review. Natalie's resume was much more impressive than mine, yet the board accepted both of us. Now, the previous Children's Directors had received some small stipend from the church, but the board decided that Natalie should be a volunteer and denied any type of remuneration for her work. This was fine with us, as she had not sought out this position. When she found out, after we left the church, that all the other directors were paid, she felt insulted after the fact.

Almost immediately, we were tasked with planning and executing upcoming outreach activities, even those that did not fall under the Children's Department. We had Easter coming up, then Mother's Day, followed by VBS and Halloween. Historically, our church would sponsor a large gathering on our property on the weekend before Easter. We had a large hill where we could put up booths and hold games for the children to get candy. While this event would typically bring over 2000 children to our property, it would result in very few people expressing interest in our church. Like many of our outreach events, this seemed to be more about appearances than building relationships within our community.

The Board decided to forego our traditional Easter event, especially considering Covid concerns. Rhonda asked about possibly doing something else, and we came up with our Spring Blessing event. Rhonda had a lot of small flower vases and was great at getting local stores to donate to the church. She was able to procure flowers from a local vendor, and the church raised another $200 for flowers and other items. On April 9th, we hosted our event. We invited people to come in and make up two small vases, one for them and one for a friend. We had our youth group on the main road, in front of the church, with signs inviting the public to come in and join us. When the mail lady arrived to deliver, I invited her inside as well. We handed out over 100 vases to the public, with many coming in only because they saw our kids holding signs. We had vases, flowers, ribbons, and even cards and other decorative items for them to create their vases. In addition to all of this, we had contact cars set out for people to connect with us. We had just enough left over to build additional vases for the women at the Rose of Sharon, a small church that met inside our sanctuary. The event was an enormous success.

Pastor Chuck and Rhonda left at the end of the month. Chuck will insist that he did not retire and that he simply stepped down from the leadership of this church. On the last Sunday in April, we had a celebration of Chuck's leadership at Federal Way Church of the Nazarene, honoring him for his leadership and Rhonda for the work she did alongside him. Rhonda had been the receptionist at the church, sat in many roles within the denomination, and was happy to help with every event hosted by the Women's and Children's ministries.

She has such a servant's heart, as does Chuck, and an endless supply of energy and love for others. It was an emotional goodbye for everyone.

Within the Nazarene Church, when a pastor leaves, it is up to the Board to determine the next steps for the church. They will work closely with the District Superintendent to make these decisions. They have three options for the interim period until a new pastor is called. They can hire a service to provide an interim pastor to serve, look to the denomination to provide pulpit supply, or they can manage everything from within. Our church decided to have pastor Shawn provide pulpit supplies, pastor Pat would be responsible for pastoral counseling, and the Board would run all other aspects of the church. Shawn is a friend of mine that I have known since 2014. He was a Baptist pastor before coming to Federal Way and helped to plant a church locally at a senior mobile home park with some of the members of Federal Way. During Covid, his church shuttered its doors and returned to Federal Way. On Sundays, he would deliver a sermon to the congregation.

During the service, when they announced this, our Youth Director looked at me and asked why I was not given some role in the church. I told him that the Board had decided that this would be our path going forward and that they had my full support. I did not want to rack any boats here, so I tried to verbally support the Board during this time. It was stressful enough without having anyone trying to challenge them during this time. I did not agree with their decisions, but I had no say in the matter. Not long after this, I had a few people ask me who Pat was and how to contact her. I would politely point her out to them. At one of our Ministry Leader meetings, it came up that someone had suggested Pat reach out to a member who was not doing well. Pat said, "If they need to talk to me, they can contact me." Wow!

In March, Natalie and I attended MinCon with some other members of the church. While there, we met Trey, who was the founder of SPARK and Equip to Engage. This is a Nazarene ministry looking to equip children and youth leaders to better engage with their kids. The convention was great, and meeting Trey was a huge thing for us. SPARK was hosting an event in May, over in Leavenworth, which would draw Nazarenes from Eastern Washington. Natalie and I met some nice people there but were stumped by a certain attitude – they only believed in working with other Nazarene churches. Natalie and I would seek out other churches to partner with, despite their denominational affiliation, but that seems to be a foreign concept in the Nazarene Church. Either way, we had a great weekend.

Right before the Spark event, I accepted a new role with a new company. I seem to change jobs every couple of years now. I had already scheduled my time off to attend the SPARK event, so I made my last day the Wednesday of that week. While on our drive out to the event, I received a call from a potential employer about scheduling an interview with me. I told them that I was starting a new job on Monday, so I would have to pass. The recruiter tried to talk me into accepting the interview, but I had already given my word to this new company. It would not be right to now accept another interview with someone else. Eventually, he got my point and wished me well. Had they contacted me earlier, I had applied for the position almost 2 months earlier. I might have been willing to take the interview. If a company finally responds to you two months after you apply, with no communication in between, what does this say about them?

Natalie was helping to establish and grow the Special Education Department with Cascade Christian Schools. She was receiving training in new systems to help identify and quantify the performance of her students to gauge their growth. It was an effective system, but sadly, it prevented her from spending as much time with the kids as she wanted to because she was constantly evaluating their growth. As a result of this, she would step away from Cascade at the end of the school year. This would allow her to spend more time developing our Children's program despite having no kids in the church.

I started my new position on May 9th. I was hired as the Assistant Plant Production Manager in the industrial laundry industry. I was going to work for the second-largest company in the United States. They have an amazing process to get everything done. Most of their accounts are weekly. This means that what comes in only has a few days to be sorted, laundered, sorted again, and ready for delivery. They do it all in less than four days. The driver goes out to make their delivery and pick up dirty items. Those come back and are sorted by the receiving team. As they are sorting, they are placing items in large bags, aiming for a target weight, which are then slung up and sorted onto lines by laundry type. These items are then "dropped" from these lines to make enough for the industrial machines. Then, they are washed, transferred to a mobile conveyor, and then put into the dryers. After being dried, they transfer into carts and go to the presses and tunnel, where the drying process is finished. From there, they go through an initial sort, separating garments by route and onto lines up above. This is all typically done on the day after they are picked up.

The second day after picking up, those lines are brought down one at a time and scanned into a computer sorting system, which separates them based on the stop, locker, and garment type. This puts everything in order for the driver to easily deliver in a few days. From there, they go to a final inspection and packaging team, which groups them together by locker and ties them together. When they are done with their process, these garments go to a final storage area, where the drivers will retrieve them from the night before their next scheduled delivery for these accounts. So, if a route is run on Monday, it is washed and sorted on Tuesday and finally sorted and packaged on Wednesday. This leaves Thursday for any stragglers to catch up with them before being loaded Friday night for a Monday delivery. Pretty impressive. A similar process is followed for towels, mats, gloves, and other items that they launder. The main difference is that they bag and package these items only a day or two before they are drawn.

Now, when it comes to washing and drying these items, there are specific weights that they are trying to meet for maximum effectiveness with their formulas. The Mats and towels are typically slung up as close to 250 lbs. as possible. Then, five bags are placed in the washing machines. In the case of mats, they are taken out wet, rolled, and put away by color and size. For the other use items, they will go into the dryers before being bagged up and placed in pick centers. Many of these are washed and bagged one day, then picked to go out for delivery the next. It was always a struggle to keep these items in stock because some drivers and locations would try to stockpile them, which caused others to be short. In addition, some drivers overstock their customers to keep their revenue coming in on a weekly basis.

We supported 15 routes at our location and another nine at a branch location. The branch would send their items to us on an overnight delivery truck, so we had even less time to wash and return their garments. The garments are washed in a batch process. The first seven routes in each day were the first batch. The remaining eight routes were the second garment batch. Everything from the Branch was the final batch. We would wash mats and red wipers all day long. We would wash the first batch, along with some of the towels and other items, then the second batch. As part of our setup for the next day, we would load in the items from the final batch, which would be washed and ready before the tunnel and press crews showed up.

In addition to this, we needed to balance the types of materials we washed throughout the day. We were trying to ensure that everything was processed in a timely manner, but we also had to balance the types of contamination we put through our wastewater processing system. All our items had either biological or industrial contamination. Our system is designed to remove these from our water discharge, but our system could not handle an overload of either of these. If we have elevated levels of industrial contamination, solvents, grease, and oil, then the chemicals we put in our system will be less effective, or we will need to increase our chemical costs by adding more of them. The same goes for processing biologics. Our system was a reactive system rather than a proactive system. We monitored it on an hourly basis, but it would take about 2 hours to see a noticeable change. We were also subject to weekly testing and monitoring through a third-party lab. It was a lot to learn and take in. During my first month, I spent a few days with our transfer driver, dropping off and picking up at the Branch location. I learned a lot during this time.

Pastor Chuck encouraged me to apply for my district license in September. I was not sure how I felt about this, as I had been having a few issues with the Board at the church. In June, I asked for a sit down with the Board Secretary, Ken D, and the Men's Ministry leader, Scott B. I had known Scott for years and considered him a friend, while Ken had something against me, although I had no idea what it was. We met up one morning at the local Panera's. The purpose of the meeting was to see if I had the Board's support to move forward with my application and, if not, what I could do to garner their support. During the meeting, Ken asked me what I thought a local license was for. I gave him the Nazarene Manual answer, but the two of them disagreed. They saw it as nothing more than an "atta-boy" for being involved with ministry. They asked me a few more questions about which parts of pastoral ministry I enjoyed most, but I left that meeting knowing that I did not, and would not, have their support if Ken oversaw the Board. And Jesus said to them, "A prophet is not without honor, except in his hometown and among his relatives and in his own household" (Mark 6:4). This kept coming to mind over the next few weeks and months. In fact, this same verse would be repeated to me by several people over the next few years.

In August, Natalie was granted an interview with Brooklake Christian School. She had applied to be the recess leader for the school. She met with the principal, who offered her the job before Natalie even walked out. The school had been struggling to fill this position, and the principal saw something in Natalie that she could not put her finger on, but she knew that God had sent her. Natalie began this new position and quickly identified a few things they needed for the role. Many of those who provided lunch and recess duty were young people, barely out of school themselves. Natalie began working to establish a process for the monitors, which the school signed off on. In addition to this, her earlier training in building the Special Education Department at Cascade helped her to identify and convince the principal that this was needed at Brooklake. Natalie introduced the staff to the process and benefits of the Dibbles testing method.

In October, a mass email was sent out to the Production Managers and Assistant Production managers about a couple of new positions opening. They were for the Production Manager position in Oklahoma City. I spoke with my wife about it. Natalie was open to the idea, so I approached my Production Manager about it as well. I knew that I was technically not eligible for the position. As a salaried employee, I had to be with the company for 12 months before I could apply for a new position. She told me to go ahead and apply, but not to get my hopes up for it. Our Regional Plant Manager reached out to me and told me how horrible the situation was in Oklahoma City. He tried to discourage me from applying, but for some reason, I felt drawn to this job. I could not explain it at the time.

It was at Brooklake that Natalie met the granddaughter of the principal. Right before Thanksgiving, the principal approached Natalie to see if we would be able to take this young lady in a few days. She had been renting a room from another teacher, and things had become unsafe for her to stay there. Because it was only supposed to be for a few days, Natalie and I agreed to take her in. Before we knew it, this young lady had become a fixture in our family. She would ride to work with Natalie every day, and we dropped her off at church with her grandma on Sundays. What was supposed to be a few days quickly turned into more than a month. That year, for our family picture with Santa, we had a new member with us.

In December, I had a series of phone interviews for the position in Oklahoma City. I met with the General Manager on the first one and then the Regional Vice President and Regional Plant Manager on the second one. The GM told me that he had four candidates, two of which were internal to the company. For some reason, he decided to offer me the position, and the offer included a lucrative relocation package. They wanted me to start in January. This meant that Natalie and I would be moving in winter again. It also meant that we had to do something about our guest in the house. We let her know, as soon as we knew, that the house was going to be listed and that she would need to find somewhere else to live. I am not sure if she did not believe us or not, but she moved out on Christmas day. Earlier that month, Natalie and I had begun packing up our house, getting ready for the move.

We also tendered our resignations at Federal Way Church of the Nazarene, which were gladly accepted. They were happy to be rid of me, and Ken's wife had been gunning for Natalie's position for a few months, which she was extremely happy to relinquish. Our last service with this church was on Christmas Day, which was anything but a service. Pastor Pat sat in the sanctuary, making herself available to any congregants who came in, but no worship or sermon was offered.

2023 – Oklahoma

Our move to Oklahoma was a nightmare, to say the least. As part of the relocation package, we were offered to have a moving company contracted by the relocation company, pack up and move our stuff, but that would take up the entire amount offered for the move. It would not include the transportation of our vehicles, our transportation, or even hotel stays until we find a place to live. We opted to look into finding our own movers. We found one that offered an acceptable estimate. When they came to pack up the house, they were not prepared. They were under the impression that they were simply loading boxes from the house and then leaving. They went out to pick up boxes and then spent the next several hours packing up some of our items. Once they began loading the truck, they had their boss call me and tell me that the estimate would be double what they had quoted. They had fit in less than half of our stuff at this point. I was furious because they had us over the fire. We had about 10 days before I needed to report to work, leaving us no time to find an alternative.

Natalie and I had already rented a small trailer to take with us, but now we needed to get a much larger trailer. That proved to be a struggle since we were moving interstate. We eventually found one, but it would not fit everything left behind. Just like when we left California, we ended up giving away many items that would not fit, including my smoker and barbeque. Natalie's Volvo and my motorcycle were left behind, to be picked up later by the moving company. Natalie and I had planned for our housekeeper to come in to do a deep clean on the house, and our real estate agent had planned for a landscaper to come in to make our yard look amazing. She just needed us to be out of the house when all of this happened.

Natalie and I left on January 14th. We loaded up into my Jeep with our two dogs and headed off to Boise, Idaho. We would spend our first night on the road with my cousin and her family. It was an 8-hour drive to their house. Spending time with family before moving completely away from family was exactly what we needed. Natalie and I were nervous about moving over to the Rockys in January, but I could not let Natalie know this.

We left Boise early the next day, the 15th, and made it as far as Moab. This was not the course we had originally planned on, but at a truck stop in Utah, while looking at a map on the wall, a stranger approached us and recommended that we take what appeared to be a more treacherous path – mostly back roads. He told us about the state of the roads to the north and about those further south. The safest route, according to this local rancher, would be our path moving forward. We made it to Moab, Utah, before I finally reached a point where I needed to stop for the night.

On the 16th, we woke up and continued our journey. Natalie and I continued on back roads and entered New Mexico. During this stretch of the trip, we would hit many hills and climb through the mountain passes. At one point, after leaving Albuquerque, we hit some areas where, according to the temperature on my Jeep, it was as low as 13 degrees outside. There were huge puddles on the ground, but none of them had frozen over. There was no ice on the road at all. It was amazing that God had sent an angel to guide us and then provided safe passage on that road despite the weather around us. This trip took us to Moriarty, New Mexico. The next day took us through Texas, to Elk City, Oklahoma. I knew that we were only a couple of hours to Oklahoma City, but I was so tired and sore from driving these last few days that I simply needed to find a place to sleep.

The next day, we arrived in Oklahoma City. Our first stop was to unload the trailer and then find a place to stay for the immediate future. Again, God decided to bless us at the storage unit. Because we had rented a trailer to move, we were entitled to a storage unit, free of charge, for a month. We went down and began to unload our trailer. After a while, I determined that we needed either a slightly larger unit or a second unit. I went back to the office to inquire about this, and due to something in their system, they gave us a second unit, right next to the first, at no charge for a month. Wow! All of our stuff fit inside these two, and still had room to maneuver items and find something if we needed to. After this, we went to find a hotel, until we could find a place to live.

We swung by the facility where I would be working to meet the GM and Office Manager. It was a nice visit, and they were kind enough to recommend some areas to look for an apartment or house to rent. After this, Natalie and I went to find a hotel for a brief time. We ended up staying at the Extended Stay off I40. This was an interesting place. You needed to scan your room card to enter that front desk area and then again to enter the main complex. It turns out that many of their residents seemed to be down on their luck, possibly addicts. Based on the level of security for the building and some things said to me by the staff, this was more probable than just possible. While Natalie was walking with Amanda, our Belgian Malinois, to take her outside to use the restroom, one of the gentlemen in the hall made a comment about how he used to have a dog like her. It made Natalie extremely nervous. We began looking for a house to rent because of the dogs. Because of the dogs, many would not rent to us. Many rental agencies denied us because of either one of the breeds, Micah is a Rottweiler Pug mix, or because of Amanda's size, she weighs 50 lbs. Eventually, we found a cute little house in the Adventure District. This is an area just north of where I was going to be working. It was close to several museums and the Science Center. The rent was right, and the backyard was huge, giving the dogs a lot of work to run around. The owner was willing to allow us to make a partial payment and then catch up on the rest after I got paid in a week. This was a blessing from God, and we knew it.

That first weekend in Oklahoma City, Natalie and I attended the 8th Street Nazarene Church. My former pastor at Guidestone Church, Doug G, had recommended it to us. Being from Oklahoma, Doug was familiar with the pastor of that church, Chris P. Natalie, and I decided to check them out. Each month, the church puts the names of restaurants in a bowl and then has the members draw one. They had different members of the staff who would be at each one, and this would be an opportunity for members and guests to get to know the staff and each other better over a meal. We ended up at the one where the senior pastor would be. He and his wife were surprised to hear that Natalie and I had just arrived three days earlier and were already looking for a church. We explained that being part of a church and having consistent attendance were important to both of us and was non-negotiable for us. It was an enjoyable meal for us despite having already decided that this was not the church for us. Chris took my contact information and later wrote an email to introduce me to Mark L, the District Superintendent of Southwest Oklahoma District, and Terry Rowland, the DS of the Oklahoma District. I never heard anything from Terry, but I did hear back from Mark a brief time later. He invited Natalie and me out to breakfast with him and his wife.

Our second weekend in Oklahoma City was spent with the members of Fifth Street Baptist Church. Our experience here was, in most ways, the exact opposite of what we experienced at 8th Street. This is an African American congregation. We were the only white couple in the sanctuary, but this was nothing new to us, and we were secretly hoping for a recreation of our time at Seed of Life. During their warmup, one of the ladies of the church came over to introduce herself and welcome us to Fifth Street. It was not until the sermon began that Natalie and I began to feel uncomfortable. Their preacher on this day was a man who was celebrating the first anniversary of his ordination. His sermon was centered around the unlawful beating of a person of color by four policemen. While he did mention that those four policemen were also black, he blamed the white man for creating a system that encourages blacks to commit such heinous violence against other black men. The gist of his sermon was that it is the duty of all minorities to stand up against white people and take charge of their own lives, even if it means killing white people. I was so incredibly uncomfortable during this "sermon" of hate I would have walked out if Natalie had not been with me. I was not sure that we would not be attacked if we tried to walk out, so we sat through this vile message and left as soon as it was over. This was my introduction to racism in Oklahoma.

When I would tell people at work where we lived, they all looked at me like I was crazy. At first, I could not understand it. It was a cute neighborhood and was close to work. It turns out that we lived in a district where the color of our skin made Natalie and I stand out. In fact, after visiting Fifth Street, Natalie became hyper-aware of this and began to feel as though all our neighbors were looking at her with the same type of hatred that the preacher expressed. It made her uncomfortable and ashamed, but the PTSD from that one experience was getting to her.

Back in December, after accepting this new position, I went online to look at houses in the Oklahoma City area. Just south of there, I found that the same company that built our house in Puyallup was also building a neighborhood. We looked at the floorplans and found one that we really liked. We filled out the interest form online, and a sales rep soon reached out to us. He took us on a tour of the floorplan we were interested in and then drove around town to show us around a little bit. It was great. The only problem was that our house was not under contract yet, let alone listed, so they really could not help us at this time. There were only two houses with the floor plan we liked left. Oh well.

The general sales manager called us in February to see if we were still interested. I had second thoughts. I really enjoyed my 10-minute commute, but our rental had some type of mold, which was making Natalie sick. She and I decided to at least go down and look at the homes but did not expect to buy there. We went down on Saturday and looked around the neighborhood and town. Amazingly, the same two houses that were available at the beginning of December were still available. Not only this, but the price had just dropped another $10k. It would mean that I would have about a 30-minute commute, but it was also far enough away from the city that we would not be subjected to many of the problems one sees in the city. We signed on the dotted line.

Our house was finally listed in Washington, and Natalie's car was finally delivered to Oklahoma. My motorcycle was not included because the transporter could not figure out how to load it and get it here. I was furious as I had already paid for this. I took my birthday off so that Natalie and I could go register our vehicles and get our Oklahoma driver's licenses. On the way there, Natalie took a wrong turn and ended up heading away from where she wanted to be. Now, there are many divided roadways in Oklahoma. Some of the greenbelts on these divisions are higher than the drivers in the vehicles. As Natalie approached one intersection, an older gentleman pulled in front of her from her left side. He had taken off from a stop sign and continued through the division without stopping or even slowing to see if there was oncoming traffic.

His front passenger side collided with Natalie's front driver side. Both cars were dead at this point, and luckily, no one was hurt. Because I needed to start a claim on our insurance, I could not switch it over to Oklahoma-specific coverage, which meant that we could not register either vehicle. This also meant that Natalie had no vehicle unless she took me to work and picked me up every day.

Our house in Washington was listed and sold virtually the same day. Within a few hours of the listing going live, we had three offers on it. Natalie and I talked about the three offers and decided to pick one. It was a young family, just starting out, and we saw it as a way to bless someone else as God had blessed us. However, overnight, they decided to withdraw their offer as they did not think that we would pick them up. We went with the next offer, which had the least restrictions. Our home closed shortly after this, which began our journey to purchase our new home, the same one we liked back in December. With some of the proceeds from our house, Natalie and I purchased a new Jeep for us. It was not perfect, but it was ours, and it was paid off. God is good!

The other house, there were two with this floor plan if you remember, sold one week after we signed on the dotted line for our own. Our move-in date was March 6th, 2023, 8 years to the day after I moved into the apartment I was in when I met Natalie. I gave notice to our landlord and offered to pay him rent through the end of April because of breaking our lease. This meant more trailer rentals and a closeout of our storage units. Because we were moving to Newcastle, Natalie and I began looking at churches in that area. The first one we found was Tri-City Cowboy & Country Church with pastor Randy H. It was a good church with a wonderful congregation, but it was not quite the perfect fit for Natalie and me. We tried it out for a little over a month but then began looking again.

The weekend before we moved into our new house, Natalie and I attended a seminar at the Mustang Church of the Nazarene. It was focused on mobilizing the church to be more involved with their communities through outreach efforts. Mark L had suggested it, and it was wonderful. I reached out to Mark about Lifespring Church of the Nazarene, which was supposed to be in Newcastle. It turns out that they are. They meet on Sunday evenings in the library. They had all four members. Natalie and I continued to look at different churches until some time in May. It was then that, based on a question from her father, we checked out Newcastle Christian Church. Pastor Billy leads this congregation, which is mostly older. Natalie and like Billy and Michelle, his wife. We began attending regularly and even going to their Wednesday night Bible study. It took us about 5 minutes to get there, which was a welcome change from Washington.

Things at work were getting insane. I am no longer sure of the timelines here; I was working six days a week and 10-12 hours per day. The company pays lower wages but well above the state minimum wage. Because all the work is essentially manual labor, they run through employees quickly, especially during the summer hours. At one point, we measured the temperature inside the building at 102 degrees, and the only cooling available were fans placed throughout the facility. Most of the employees in the warehouse were either African

American or Hispanic. Now, the Spanish word for black is *Negra.* One of the African American employees overheard some of the Hispanic women talking and caught this word in their conversation. Thinking that they were using a racial epithet, he raised a concern with the office manager, which initiated an investigation. This was not the first time something like this had happened, nor was it the last time. I began to feel that the Office Manager had something against Hispanics between this and other events. She also had something against many of the hourly employees in the warehouse, but she had been there so long that she ran the place. In Oklahoma City, there is some major issue between many of the African Americans and Hispanics, to the point of violence. Some of the other incidents that happened while I was with this company include me and my assistant being physically assaulted by a drunk employee, having to terminate several employees for showing up smelling like they had just smoked marijuana, and even terminating employees for leaving the work site without clocking out.

One of the worst incidents happened in late summer or early fall. In Washington, we had one branch location, but here we had two. One of my drivers was very friendly with some of the women at the plant. This made other women jealous, for lack of a better term, who would report him for sexually harassing those he was friends with. One day, he was in a bad mood, and he got into a verbal argument with one of the ladies who did not like him very much. Words were exchanged between the two. He admitted to saying something very disrespectful and criminal to the lady. I suspended him on the spot and allowed the company to perform their investigation of the event. The result of that investigation was to terminate his employment with the company. He was a nice guy and someone I could have a good relationship with, but misogyny has no place in the world today.

Non-employee-related issues included upgrading our sorting system, which led to issues and manual fixes, a busted water main because the city switched pumps without shutting one down first, ongoing mechanical issues with our equipment, and a culture of backstabbing and actively working against one another. It was not a healthy work environment. I must be careful about what I write here because I have been under an NDA with the company for a couple more years. The less said beyond this, the better.

In May, my paternal grandmother passed away. It was bittersweet for me. I had seen her a year earlier when my stepfather passed. Our visit was a good one. I got to tell her about me going to school to be a pastor, about some of the exciting things God was doing in our lives, and, best of all, she knew who I was. Grandma had advanced Alzheimer's. Some days were good, others were bad. My aunt had a routine with her. She would show her pictures from grandma's life, reminding her of who was in the pictures, and then brush her hair and just talk to her. I got to do this with her. Not only did Grandma recognize me while I was there, but my aunt told me that Grandma remembered my visit the next day. That was an exceptionally good day.

They had Grandma's memorial service in June. I drove out to California. It was supposed to be a straight shot – out I 40 and then across the I 10. Well, in Santa Rosa, my Jeep decided to overheat. I was stuck in traffic because of a fatality several miles down the highway. Traffic was at a standstill. Jeep overheated, but I got off the highway safely and called a tow truck. They got me back to the shop, but it would not be ready until the next day. I stayed at a hotel for the night and then walked to a local church while I was waiting for the repair shop. They got my jeep fixed, and I headed out. I made it about two miles before it overheated again. The original problem was a stuck thermostat. This time, it was a broken overflow tank, which allowed the heated coolant to run out onto the ground. A couple more hours and I was back on the road. This time, I made it to California.

Once in California, I stayed at the same hotel as I always did. It was low rent, but I am cheap. I met with family, many of whom I had not seen in a couple of decades. I took one last spin around my grandparents' house, and then we went to the viewing. Ran into a few more family friends, but it was a highly emotional affair for me. My grandma was the last person tying me to California. The next day, we all drove out to the Veteran's Cemetery in Riverside. Grandma would be interred there with Grandpa. On the drive out, I was disturbed by how much the area had been built up since I was last there. Now, there are buildings and developments right up to the cemetery. Most of SoCal is now an urban jungle. No wonder it is always so dang hot. When I left for home, I brought with me a family portrait from before I was born, but I was still in the portrait, and a quilt frame. I was happy to have those two items.

In August, Natalie went to work for the Norman School District as a para for their Special Education classrooms. While there, she made some friends and grew even more determined not to return to the classroom as a teacher. Many of their policies and procedures were not comfortable for her. She was assaulted on an almost daily basis by the students, yet she still loved working with the kids, even those who did not know how to behave. I think the worst part for her, though, was the commute. There are only two main ways in and out of Newcastle to either Oklahoma City or Norman. My route took me east, which was easy in the morning but packed at night. Her route also took her east but on a different highway. The intersection from that highway to the next in Norman is under construction, and it gets worse every day. It did not help that she was at the school furthest from our house, which meant a 30-minute commute for her.

I was still enrolled in Nazarene Bible College, sort of. My last classes were in January 2023 and then picked up again in August 2023. I was scheduled to do my Supervised Ministry Experience during both sessions, but I canceled the one in January because I would have had to do it remotely with pastors Shawn and Pat. I was uncomfortable with this. I finished out the Winter 2022 block in February and waited until August to begin what I thought would be my final block. I wanted to be established with a local church before working on the Ministry Experience. It only took a week to realize that I would not be able to do this at Newcastle, so I dropped it while finishing the other two classes. *Leading the People of God* and *Preaching the Story of God* were finished by the end of 2023.

Supervised Ministry Experience would need to wait until later. The reason for this is that I would need to have not only a mentor but also a Congregational Support Team, and I would need to be more involved with the activities and leadership of the church. I did not feel that I could do this at Newcastle.

Natalie's parents, Gene and Cecilia, moved in with us on November 1st. Natalie's sister, Rita, had decided to sell her home in Maricopa and move to Arkansas to be closer to her cousin. As Gene and Cecelia had been living with her since their return to the States, this meant that they would need to find a new place to live. Natalie and I had anticipated this, which is why we bought such a large house. We took them to the Tri-City church and Newcastle Christian. They had issues with each of them and wanted to try to find one on their own. Eventually, they settled as Newcastle Christian. As we finished out 2024, Natalie and I began talking about trying to find a Nazarene church that could help me with this last class.

2024 – Blessings from God

This year began with much trepidation and concern. We had gotten a new GM at work back in September. In one of his first meetings with me, he asked a question that showed me how short a time I had left – Are you on board with my vision? I was, but I was not sure what it all meant. He had ends in mind, but I am not sure he knew what the journey would look like to get there. Add to this my growing frustration with work conditions, it would all come to a final decision soon.

At the end of January, I reached out to Pastor Nate, the pastor at Mustang Nazarene. I asked if he had time for me to meet with him. I wanted to ask if he would be willing to help me with my *Supervised Ministry Experience.* That first Sunday, I met with Steve D., a board member. We talked about it, and he introduced me around. The following week, Nate called to say that he would be happy to help with this. Natalie and I began attending Mustang that last weekend in January.

I had planned to take a couple of days off for my birthday in February. Natalie and I were looking forward to going to Kansa City for the weekend and visiting some of her friends. One of the things we did at work was to print off pictures and motivational quotes of African Americans and post them around the site in honor of Black History Month. While in the breakroom, taking a break, I saw a picture of Jackie Robinson. I exclaimed aloud that I could not wait to see the *Negro League Museum* in Kansa City this week. I did not realize that an employee was in the room, but he took exception with my use of the word Negro, despite it being the actual name of the league and the museum. He reported me to the Office Manager and GM, who suspended me since I was on vacation for the next 2 days anyway. This was just getting ridiculous. Natalie and I went to Kansas that night.

We stopped off along the way, then went to MidAmerican Nazarene and the Nazarene Global Center the next day before finishing our trip just outside of Kansas City. We got to visit her friends at work. They teach in a small Christian college. We were invited to join them for their chapel service. It was in this chapel service that we heard about their theology club meeting that afternoon. We were told we could attend, so we did. I had planned on just listening, but there are times that God has other plans. The club meeting was fun, and many of the students, and even the faculty, seemed interested in what I had to share with them. They learned a little about my background, which was completely foreign to all of them. When it was over, I was invited to come back sometime so that I could host a discussion panel. That is exciting. We spent the rest of the weekend with Natalie's friends and then drove back.

Upon our return to Newcastle, I reached out to the GM to see what to do. He said he was still waiting for a word from HR and asked me to be patient. I was good with that. He eventually called me Monday afternoon, asking if I would prefer to come in this afternoon or wait until the following morning after the employees had started. I opted for the morning. When I got there, we went into his office. He had a surprisingly good offer for me: the company would allow me to leave immediately with no financial obligation to the company, but I would never be allowed to work for them again and could never say anything derogatory about the company or their employees for a period of three years. I was good with this, and it was another blessing from God. Had they not let me leave this way, or had they decided to fire me, I would have had to pay back the relocation allowance, which was more than I could afford. God was allowing me to leave a situation that was not healthy for me with no repercussions to speak of. God is good!

Mustang Nazarene is under the leadership of pastor Nathan Burns (Nate). Nate will tell you that it is the Holy Spirit who leads this church, and I would agree with him about this. It is also the Holy Spirit that brought Nate here to help teach and model what it means to be led by the Holy Spirit.

Nate is a pastor's kid, so he has that in common with Natalie. He is also a Nazarene, through and through. Nate lives according to the Nazarene Manual and tries to glorify Christ in all that he does. This shows through in his congregation and leadership team. Mustang Naz has a quite simple mission statement: Love Above All. This means that they Love Everyone, Every Day, Everywhere, above all else. And they do. Nate always says, "No one prays alone at Mustang Naz." Natalie noticed this during his sermons, so she paid attention to see if this was just the talk or if the church walked the walk. They do. Week after week, we would see people come to the altar for prayer, even us. Every time, people would get up and leave their seats, even when they did not know who the person kneeling, just to pray with them for God's favor in their lives. It was not just fluff in this church. They put action to words.

Natalie and I tried a couple of different Sunday School groups. We settled on the Connections class, led by Brent. I did not know it at the time, but Brent would become a dear friend of mine, and I do not use that word lightly. Brent is a schoolteacher with advanced degrees in the biomedical field. He has a long history in Oklahoma and has a wonderful wife, Wanda, and two awesome girls. The youngest is still at home.

The Connections class is not your typical Sunday School group. We do life together often. Some of our discussions will go down serious rabbit holes, but that is where we need to go to help someone in the group with what they are dealing with. Natalie and I had been in Brent's class for a couple of weeks when he announced that he was going to fill in for pastor Nate at Arbor House. Arbor House is an assisted living facility in Mustang. We asked where it was so that we could join Brent there and support him. Natalie and I still laugh when we think about a senior assisted living facility being located on Cemetery Road, but there it is.

That Sunday, Brent gave his testimony. I cannot remember if he told us before this event, but Brent has a rare form of cancer. He was getting ready to head down to a facility in Houston for stem cell treatment. They had no idea if this would help him or hurt him, but Brent was approved for the treatment. I got to hear about his past and current struggles that day. It affected me on a deep level.

Natalie and I continued to attend the Connections class and Arbor House. We went to support pastor Nate and anyone else he had preaching that weekend. At one point, Nate had something else that he needed to do, so he asked if I could fill in at Arbor House. I agreed to this, and Natalie and I continued to attend. Then, the church suffered a major blow – a member of the church passed away at an early age. This member was close to Nate, and he took it hard. I approached Nate and asked if he wanted me to cover Arbor House for him so that he could go and grieve with the family. He took me up on this.

It was the next week, upon his return to Arbor House, that Nate asked me if I would head up the ministry there. I agreed. As I was out of work now, I was able to visit the residents during the week. I met some wonderful people, who I grew to love as family members. I began preaching every weekend, and eventually, my wife began leading praise and worship. We never thought we would be in this type of position, and it has brought us a lot of joy in getting to know everyone. The hardest part is that this is an assisted living facility, which means that, on occasion, our residents will be called home to Jesus. Losing a friend is always hard.

In the Connection class, Natalie and I met many people. We have been blessed to learn about their struggles and to pray alongside them. I would like to highlight just a few of the ones that stand out, but for their own anonymity, I am going to use initials rather than names.

MW is a wonderful young lady with a heart for kingdom work. She and SB run the Fostering Our Village ministry. This is an amazing ministry that seeks to provide clothing and other items at no charge to those in need. They have served thousands of children since revitalizing this ministry in 2024. MW sees those who are often overlooked by society. What was once established to specifically help foster families has grown to provide for the needs of anyone who comes. MW also comes out of a particular group, which many claim is a cult, and has faced adversity in leaving that group, yet God brought her family and ours together. She recently relocated out of the country, too soon for Natalie, but we can stay connected through social media and letters.

AS and KS are a couple in the connections class. Both have military backgrounds, and both support another ministry of the church – RWOL (Restoring Wholeness of Life). This is a local CrossFit gym where they work out. It is a ministry started by BA, who moved to Hermosa Beach to plant a church. They seek to increase the health of their members through both physical and spiritual activity.

Mustang Naz supports one of our local school districts, Western Heights, and we help to provide food for the football team before every game. This year, we began to host them at our church the night before the game. The last week of the season, this fell on Halloween. KS was the speaker for this. Her experience as a Drill Instructor/Sergeant allowed her to speak into these boys' lives. She related her passion for seeing new recruits succeed to that of their coaches seeing them succeed. It brought back a lot of memories for me, hearing her speak about boot camp with the passion she has.

This was followed up a couple of weeks later, with AS sharing part of his testimony with the Connections class. When I first asked if he would be willing to speak, he did not think that his story would take that long or be interesting. I can honestly say that all of us were riveted to listen to him, and he even ran a little long. The only part that was missing was that moment when Jesus finally got his attention.

RR is another member of our class. He was the second person to share his testimony. His testimony is a hard one. He has been through so much and suffered at the hands of those who should love him. Yet today, he is married to a wonderful woman and has two amazing little kids. His story is a story of God pursuing him, past the point of exhaustion, and into redemption. It is a story that we all should share in.

CM is another pastor at the church. Her story is heartbreaking at some points, and yet at others, you cannot help but see the hand of God in her life. She is currently working with several members of the congregation to get a Celebrate Recovery group started at the church, works full-time for a ministry at another church, and is enrolled in her higher education program for her master's degree. I have no idea how she manages to get it all done, but she does.

In addition to these and other members of the Connection class, we have a great staff at the church. In addition to Nate as senior pastor, we have our children's pastor, discipleship pastor, worship pastor, youth pastor, and many more. Nate's dad serves in various pastoral support roles, including leading his own classes, which just serves as proof that God is never done with us on this side of heaven. Of all of these, I have the most interaction with pastor Noah.

Pastor Noah is our youth pastor. He is a hoot. Despite being a little older than the high schoolers in his group, Noah has the heart of a big kid. He gets excited about going to concerts, is a self-proclaimed Swiftie, and plays video games. Yet he takes his role as a pastor seriously. He wants to have fun with the kids while still giving them a firm foundation in Christ. Pastor Noah and I are partnering to bring some Christmas cheer to the residents of Arbor House this year.

In April, I interviewed for three different jobs, and all of them were good. The first one made me an offer, but I was waiting for a response from one that I felt drawn to. In the meantime, I had an interview with a third job close to home, one that would certainly pay the bills. It was a very lucrative job. I received an offer from this third job, which was quickly followed by an offer from the second company. Natalie and I talked about and prayed over each of these offers. The position closest to us offered more money, $20K more, and was a 10-minute commute. The downside to it was the level of responsibility involved. They worked 6 days a week, and it seemed implied that I would be expected to be there during those days. It was a lot to ask. The other position was about 30 minutes away and paid less, but it was just 8 hours per day, Monday – Friday. This would allow me to continue to minister at Arbor House during the week and attend Wednesday night Bible study at Mustang. I ended up accepting the role with the second company.

I began my new role on April 29th. I was hired to be the Warehouse Manager at one of two Schoolbook Depositories for the State of Oklahoma. During the interview process, it was conveyed to me that I would be replacing the current warehouse manager, Chris G, who was ready to retire. It turns out that Chris has no intention of retiring and simply wants to be able to take some time off. At the time I was hired, there were two full-time and three temporary employees in the warehouse. They had just finished with replacement orders and would be receiving and shipping the new items in a few months.

Oklahoma is under an adoption cycle for its educational materials. The cycle runs for six years and is divided by subjects. Most of the time, the publishers will host a caravan for the schools around the State. During this event, my employer sent out people to help with the displays and staging of the product. The only year they do not do the caravan is when all the material is online. This is during the technology and art adoption. Through the caravan, the teachers get to review the material and decide which of the adopted items the schools want to use for the upcoming period. Orders are then placed through us with the publisher, and the materials begin to arrive during June and July. As the materials come in, we receive them and fill the orders to be sent out to the schools. It gives us a hectic few months, but nothing crazy. Then, in November, we conduct a wall-to-wall inventory of the items in the warehouse. After a couple of weeks of reconciling, we can mark the inventory complete.

During the months leading up to our regular inventory, I tried to see what we had, but the numbers just did not line up. Our Warehouse Management System (WMS) is antiquated and hard to maintain. We hold stock under different programs as well as individual items. For instance, you could have one textbook under a single item and then under different programs designed to be used when items are bought either on or off-cycle for adoption. I have seen 6-year, 5-year, 3-year, and even single-year programs. Each of these programs may have one or more items in them, and not always the same items. This makes inventory difficult to reconcile. I had one set that was made up of four different items in the 6-year program, two items in the 3-year program, and then just one item in a couple of different single-year programs. Inventory was held under all four programs and the individual item, but it was all stored in one location.

In June, our niece came to live with us. There were some issues going on at home in Florida that made life unsafe for her at home. We learned about much of this later in the year. Meanwhile, I was able to have her work with me during the summer. One of our school districts, Tulsa Public Schools, asks us to barcode their main textbooks for certain grades. This process involves applying an adhesive barcode and then a clear label over it. She enjoyed the work and enjoyed the paycheck even more.

June came, and we had a few days of work to keep us busy. In July, things picked up, and we stayed busy. By the time the middle of August rolled around, though, our busy season was all but finished. We began to lay off the temporary employees, including my niece. We had enough work to keep us busy through September. I was still visiting Arbor House twice during the week and preaching on Sundays. With the lack of work during the week, I found ample time to study and write my sermons; this would not have happened had I picked the other position. It really was a blessing from God for me.

Our niece came to live with us in the middle of June. We only had two fixed rules for her: she would attend church, and we would eat dinner as a family. This was a change for her, but she quickly grew to enjoy it. Right after she arrived, Gene and Cecelia told us that they were going to Arizona for a visit. We were fine with this, but I did scold them because Natalie's birthday was coming up, and I had a feeling that they were leaving before that. They promised Natalie that they would still be in Oklahoma to celebrate her birthday with her. They left on June 26th, four days before her birthday. I was irate with them over this. Their decision in this matter did not strain our relationship; it broke it.

In July, David, Natalie's brother, had filed a police report in Florida, claiming that Natalie and his wife had kidnapped our niece and then transported her over state lines. The local police department where he filed determined that no crime had been committed in Florida, so they sent it off to the Newcastle Polie Department. The detective there came by the house and spoke with our niece. They, too, determined that no crime had been committed, but this did not stop David from trying to do something. Fay, his wife, had him served with a summons for a Personal Protection Order hearing. He had been stalking her and sending anonymous letters to her employer, trying to get her fired. Sadly, the case was dismissed because all the evidence was circumstantial, and Fay had never filed a police report for any of the violence against her.

Gene and Cecelia had originally planned to come back to Oklahoma at the beginning of September. Right before this, they called Natalie to let us know that they were extending their trip. They did not say for how long and did not indicate that this was a permanent move for them, but Natalie and I suspected it. Shortly after this, Gene called Natalie to inform her when his flight would land so that she could pick him up at the airport. He did not ask her; he simply told her. Natalie, being the dutiful daughter, showed up at the airport to pick up Gene and some guy from Arizona. Gene took them all to lunch at his favorite dinner, where he informed Natalie that he and Mom were moving back for good. They planned to leave their stuff at our house and in their storage unit because it was cheaper and that the gentleman with him had come to drive their car back to Arizona. We suspected this, but this is still a disrespectful way for them to do this. Our relationship with them is broken, possibly forever.

Near the middle of October, our niece attended a Youth Church camp. She had been going to church with Natalie and I and had gotten to know some of the girls in the Youth group well. On Saturday evening, she reached out to Natalie. She was struggling with thoughts of self-harm. Natalie and I immediately left to go pick her up from camp. We drove her to an urgent care by the house while she talked with a friend of hers. Urgent Care could not do much and recommended that we take her to the Emergency Room. Once there, they placed her under observation because she had admitted to having suicidal thoughts. The next morning, she was transferred to the Children's Resource Center (CRC) for admission and care. Natalie and I were terrified. We thought we had failed this young lady somehow. She was admitted on Sunday and released on Monday of the following week. While she was there, she met with a counselor and learned to open up to him. She confessed to some things that had happened at home with her father. I had suspected much of this but had no corroboration of this.

During her time at CRC, Mustang Nazarene rallied around our niece. We had several pastors and members of the youth group wanting to visit her, writing cards to her, and putting together care packages for her. It was amazing to see the church be the Church. Nate and several others asked how they could help Natalie and me with everything. Once our niece was released, her mom came out for a short visit. The two of them had a wonderful time together. I spent the beginning of November, during her visit, at a conference in Tulsa. At the end of October, David had filed a motion with the courts to force the return of his daughter and to restrict Fay's rights to visitation with their daughter. In reading the filing, I noticed that there was a lot of false information and mistakes contained in his filing. True or false, it sent our niece into another spiral.

As Thanksgiving approached, Natalie and I began to get a little excited about getting our annual picture taken with our niece. She was getting worked up over what her dad was doing. The day before Thanksgiving, I got a call from Natalie. During her call with her therapist, our niece had said something that concerned her. She wanted her to be evaluated by our local emergency room and possibly readmitted to CRC. I went home and took us all to the ER. Our niece minimized it to us and the doctors. She came home later that day. Thanksgiving day passed without incident, but when we went Black Friday shopping, we could tell that something was wrong. She was struggling, and it showed. We gave her time and let her come to us when she was ready.

Fay and David had mediation scheduled for December 20th. During their mediation, it was explained to David that he had filed in the wrong municipality. He needed to file in the county he lived in. They also raised concerns over whether the State had authority over our niece because she had lived in the State for less than 3 months during the year. Oklahoma gained jurisdiction over her as of December 13th, which was the 6-month mark for her living with us. On December 26th, Fay was served with more paperwork, filed by David with the same court, demanding the return of his daughter and asking the court to enforce his request. After much discussion with Fay, Natalie and I began the paperwork for the courts in Oklahoma to establish guardianship of our niece. We did not want it to come to this, but David left us little choice. Natalie and I went to the courthouse on December 30th to file for guardianship. It pains me that we need to do this, but I will do anything I can to protect this little girl from being further harmed.

As December 2024 was wrapping up, I was getting ready for my interview with the District for my license. Part of this involved a sit down with the District Superintendent, the Ministerial Board Secretary, and Pastor Nate. We met at Mustang Nazarene and sat down to discuss my history, my call, and a little about my divorces. I was nervous, considering how this turned out the last time. I am not sure what is going to happen next, but my actual License interview is coming up on January 21st.

Christmas Eve was spent at Arbor House and Mustang Nazarene. I hosted the candlelight service at Arbor House and got to enjoy the service at Mustang. Christmas was a fun day at our house. Our niece was surprised to be as spoiled as she was. We wanted to make Christmas a fun day for her. Christmas last year was when her family imploded, so she was not looking forward to Christmas this year. Saturday night that week, I received a text from Nate about covering at a local church the next morning. Pastor Paul, from Seed of Life, had told me early on to "always have something ready," which I took to heart. When Nate texted me about the pastor being sick and needing a stand-in the next day, my immediate response was yes.

I preached on being open to those who are different from you. This church is getting ready to grow. The church is located on the outskirts of the town but still on the main highway into town. During the summer, as they were getting ready for their new pastor to come in, several of us from Mustang went to help them remodel the parsonage. While we were there, Nate had a discussion with someone and told them about our Kids Day Out (KDO) program. We were full and had several parents from the same town as this church. This prompted them to begin a KDO campus on their church grounds. In less than a year, they had fifteen students, with a 16th one coming soon. The new pastor and his wife are looking to grow the relationship of the church with their community. This leads me to believe that this church is going to grow over the next year. The pastor is a young man who has a strong heart for the Lord. Being asked to cover for him was a huge honor for me.

2025 and Beyond

Brent and I are getting ready for our District License interviews on the 21st of January. This could be the first major milestone for my journey toward ordination, or it could be a complete disaster. Because of my prior divorces, the Board may decide to pass on me this year, or they could choose to approve my continuation on this journey. Either way, I am ok with whatever they decide. Some may say that I am a bit of a legalist when it comes to what is in the Nazarene Manual, but I try to constantly live my life within the bounds laid out in it. Technically, the General Superintendents need to agree to remove my divorces as a barrier to ordination prior to me being granted my District License. They will not meet until after the decision is made by our District Credential Board meeting. So, while the District will grant new Licenses in May, it may be August before the General Superintendents would have a chance to convene and discuss me. I might have to wait until next year. The good news is that this will have no bearing on my serving either Mustang Nazarene or Arbor House.

Things with our niece are progressing. In early January, something amazing happened. She willingly gave up the instrument that she used to commit self-harm. She knocked on our door one night and handed it to Natalie, telling her, "I want to give this to you before I change my mind. I do not think I need it anymore." Praise God for this! She may not yet have a relationship with Jesus, but we see her growing closer every day.

Last year, we lost around a dozen residents at Arbor House. Many of these people I have come to know and love. I know that we will continue to lose residents. In fact, there are several that I am praying for now. It is the nature of the ministry. This does not make each loss any easier. The last one in 2024 was Roberta. She reminds me a lot of my own grandmother. She was 99 years old, a few days from her 100th birthday. She would always want to hold someone's hand. She would constantly tell me that she "loved my chin whiskers." One day in November, I received a call from Ashley, letting me know that Roberta was not doing well. I rushed over to Arbor House to see Roberta. She was struggling to breathe, so I sat with her. I held her hand while I read to her from the Gospel of John. The following night, she was up and moving like nothing was ever wrong. This was the rally before the end. On Sunday, I met her son and daughter. We talked for a few hours, them telling me about Roberta before she came to Arbor House and me listening. The next day, Roberta went home to the Lord in peace. God is good!

The fighting within my own family over the estate of my grandparents should be ending by late spring. There is a court date set for the final determination of the estate, after which they will be able to distribute it. I hate that it got to the point that it did, but thankfully, this will finally be over two years after Grandma went to heaven.

Things with Gene and Cecelia have progressed to the point that Natalie and I wrote each of them a letter. In these letters, we attempt to clarify how their actions have made both of us feel. I expressed my anger and outrage with how they treated my wife and their granddaughter. I said the things that neither of them would say to these two. I must have written that letter a dozen times before I got it all out in a way that I hope will spur action and change more than resentment. As of today, I have no idea what impact this will have on our family, but I know that God is in it with us.

Natalie and I are looking forward to another year together, experiencing the awesomeness of God in our lives and with our niece. We have some amazing friends in the members of Mustang Nazarene and Newcastle Christian. Each of us looking to continue to foster these relationships and to possibly make even more as we continue the path God has laid out before us. I have my eyes set on a particular church in our District, but that is just a pipe dream at this point. If Natalie and I have learned anything over the past 8-years, it is that God knows and God will provide. We serve an awesome God. If you are reading this and would like to know more about this amazing and awesome God, reach out to me or a pastor near you. Ask them to tell you the gospel message of Jesus Christ.

An Open Invitation

Hello,

My name is Shane, and I would like to introduce you to my best friend. But before I introduce you, I would like to tell you why he is my best friend:

You see, he is always there for me, even before I chose to acknowledge him in my life. He was there to support me, to offer me comfort, and to guide me on life's journey, even though I did not know him at the time.

He loves me unconditionally. He loves me even though I would curse him, cuss at him, and rail against him in my life prior to knowing him. He was always there, patiently waiting for me. When I was not willing or able to listen to him, he would send another to provide relief or guidance to me, knowing that I would not even acknowledge his part in it.

He loves me so much that he is available 24/7. All I need to do is reach out to him. He loves me so much that he put himself in harm's way for me before I ever knew him. He has suffered the anger of the world to protect and provide for me.

One day, when I was completely broken by loss, he approached me, making himself known to me. In that moment of desperation, he told me that it was going to be ok. I knew at that moment I was forgiven for everything I had done against him in my past.

Now, having him as my best friend does not mean that my life is now easy. In fact, it is even more difficult in some ways because he asks me to love others as he has loved me. This means that I am to show love to those who rebel against me. I am to show love to those who would spit in my face or strike me. Yet, because I know his love, it comes easier than it would have in the past.

My friend has always been around. He was there at the creation of the world, "In the beginning was the Word, and the Word was with God, and the Word was God. He was in the beginning with God. All things were made through Him, and without Him, nothing was made that was made. In Him was life, and the life was the light of men. And the light shines in the darkness, and the darkness did not comprehend it" (John 1:1-5).

My friend was sent by His Father to redeem the world, "For God so loved the world that he gave his one and only Son, that whoever believes in him shall not perish but have eternal life" (John 3:16).

My friend, Jesus, tells us, "I am the way and the truth and the life. No one comes to the Father except through me" (John 14:6).

Jesus tells us, "Anyone who has seen me has seen the Father" (John 14:9).

Here, we see that Jesus is the only begotten Son of God. That He is eternal. That He is the way, the truth, and the life. That no one may know the Father unless they know the Son and anyone who has seen the Son has seen the Father. Jesus is the second person of the Holy Trinity.

Can you imagine that the creator of the world, and everything in it, would willingly decide to divest Himself of His divinity for a time, to come and walk the earth as a human, who would then die at the hands of those He loves? Jesus did this. He is wholly Man and wholly God at the same time. He was tempted with sin, just like you and I, yet He resisted that temptation, unlike you and me.

"For God did not send his Son into the world to condemn the world, but to save the world through him" (John 3:17). He came in love to offer a path of redemption, not condemnation. The Apostle Paul tells us, "Nevertheless, I would not have known what sin was had it not been for the law" (Romans 7:7b). Jesus, in His Sermon on the Mount, corrected many of the ideas Jews held about the law (Mosaic law), by clarifying that it was just as bad to think the deed as it was to do it. Sin became a heart condition rather than just a physical action. None of us can live up to the standard of not thinking or desiring something.

So, Jesus sent us help, "I will ask the Father, and he will give you another advocate to help you and be with you forever— the Spirit of truth. The world cannot accept him because it neither sees him nor knows him. But you know him, for he lives with you and will be in you" (John 14:16-17). The Holy Spirit will always be with us, refining us into the image of Christ and will strengthen us during our times of need.

Jesus is the best friend any of us can have, and He is pursuing you just as He pursued me. Once you know Christ, your life will change. You will no longer be bound, in sin, to the desires of the world. Instead, you will be able to pursue

God's will for you in this world. Take comfort in knowing the Lord.

Chaplain Shane MacQuarrie

Chaplain to the unchurched

"Here I am! I stand at the door and knock. If anyone hears my voice and opens the door, I will come in and eat with that person, and they with me."

Revelation 3:20 NIV

Made in the USA
Columbia, SC
14 February 2025

dd3d685b-4098-4dea-a687-9e2dca38f996R01